HD 4928 .N62 U6337 1986
Foster, Ronald M.
The manager's guide to employee benefits

DATE DUE

APR 26 1994			
MAY 12 1994			
MAR 21 1996			
FEB 24 1998			

THE COMMUNITY COLLEGE OF ALLEGHENY COUNTY
ALLEGHENY CAMPUS
808 RIDGE AVENUE
PITTSBURGH, PA.
15212
LIBRARY

DEMCO

THE MANAGER'S GUIDE TO EMPLOYEE BENEFITS

How to Select and Administer the Best Program for Your Company

Ronald M. Foster, Jr.

Facts On File Publications
New York, New York • Oxford, England

The Manager's Guide to Employee Benefits

Copyright © 1986 by Ronald M. Foster, Jr.

All rights reserved. No part of this book may be reproduced or utilized in any form or by any means, electronic or mechanical, including photocopying, recording or by any information storage and retrieval systems, without permission in writing from the Publisher.

Library of Congress Cataloging-in-Publication Data
Foster, Ronald M. Jr.
  The manager's guide to employee benefits

  Bibliography: p.
  Includes index.
1. Employee fringe benefits—United States. I.
Title HD4928.N62U6337   1986   658.3'25   85-25419
ISBN 0-8160-1144-3

Printed in the United States of America
10 9 8 7 6 5 4 3 2 1

Composition by Facts On File/Circle Graphics
Printed by Maple Vail Book Manufacturing Group

CONTENTS

A Word to the Reader v

1. An Introduction to Employee Benefits 1
   Employee benefits today 1
   Why bother with benefits? 3
   Needs vs. rewards 8
   A little benefits history 10
   A changing population—and how it affects benefits . 11
   Some basic benefits principles 13

2. A Guide to Employee Benefits 15
   Time off 16
   Health insurance 29
   Other kinds of health protection 50
   Life insurance 61
   Long-term disability insurance 72
   Pensions 77
   Other retirement and
      capital-accumulation programs 98
   Special services 123
   Employment-related benefits 135
   Benefits primarily for executives 147

3. Flexible Benefits 155
   Why have a flexible benefits program? 156
   The origins of flexible benefits 157

Some basic principles 159
The arguments against flexible benefits 164
Alternate approaches to flexibility 167
Flexible benefits programs—some examples 170
A late-model program: Thomas Jefferson University 174
What about the future of flexible benefits? 177

4. Some Important Benefits Issues **179**
What will happen if benefits are taxed
   more heavily? 180
Should employees pay more of the costs? 183
Is everyone entitled to the same benefits? 186
What about post-retirement benefits? 190
How should a benefit plan be funded? 194

5. Managing Employee Benefits **199**
Keeping up to date 200
Getting feedback 202
Planning ahead 204
Handling special problems 208
Using outside help 211

6. Communicating Employee Benefits **213**
The importance of benefits communication 213
What communication can do 214
What the law requires 217
How to communicate 220
Some benefits communications principles 229

7. Benefits Resources **233**
Books 233
Periodicals 234
Organizations 236
Education 239
Government agencies 239
Benefits consultants 240
A short glossary of benefits acronyms
   and abbreviations 242

Index **246**

A WORD TO THE READER

If you are a professional employee benefits manager, you probably will be familiar with most of the contents of *The Manager's Guide to Employee Benefits*...or at least you *should* be. To tell the truth, this book wasn't designed primarily for you. But that certainly doesn't mean you should stop reading. If you keep going, you'll discover that we've tried to give a broad overview of just about every aspect of employee benefits. And it's very likely that we'll refresh your memory about some of the things you haven't thought about recently.

But the people who should find this book most useful are all those businessmen and women who haven't, until recently, paid very much attention to employee benefits. In fact, their only contact with benefits may well have been when they've used one of their own benefit plans.

Today, the planning and management of employee benefits can no longer be simply handed over to the professionals on a company's staff or to expert consultants hired from the outside. Like it or not, benefits have become too important—too costly—for that. This means, then, that the following people should get the most out of *The Manager's Guide to Employee Benefits*:

- executives or owners of small companies who are starting to feel that they should know a lot more about employee

benefits—especially when they are spending so much money on them;
- middle managers in large or medium-size firms who, without any previous experience in the field, suddenly have acquired responsibility for their companies' benefits programs; and, in fact,
- any businesspeople who've come to realize that some basic grounding in benefits management can add an extra dimension to their backgrounds—something that isn't acquired in most formal business administration programs.

How the Book Is Organized

Chapter 1 deals with some prime considerations that, all too often, don't get the attention they deserve: Why should a company have a benefits program in the first place and, if a company *does* offer benefits (as is very probably the case), what should be their real objectives?

Chapter 2—by far the largest part of the book—presents some basic information about almost every conceivable kind of employee benefit, ranging from the most common, such as health insurance and pensions, to some, such as child care and legal expenses, that relatively few companies now provide. In dealing with most of these benefits, we have tried to go beyond the basic facts and figures—and to discuss some of the more controversial of today's benefits problems. Under health insurance, for instance, we give a good bit of space to the pros and cons of cost containment. And, in discussing pensions, we weigh the relative merits of defined-benefit and defined-contribution plans.

Chapter 3 covers in considerable depth one topic of fast-growing importance: flexible benefits programs. We explain why those may represent the most important current development in employee benefits planning—and the problems that must be solved by companies that want to move toward flexible benefits.

In Chapter 4 we bring up a few of the basic issues that concern the whole field of employee benefits, not just the various individual plans. We discuss such overriding problems as the proposed new taxation of benefits, deciding how employers and employees should share the costs of benefits, and what kind of benefits a company should offer to its retired employees.

Chapter 5 takes our treatment of benefits one step further. We go beyond planning and setting up new benefit plans and discuss long- and short-range benefits planning, as well as how to handle the day-to-day operation of an ongoing benefits program.

Chapter 6 is devoted to one aspect of management responsibility—benefits communication—that can be essential to the success of both a newly introduced benefit plan and a continuing program.

Finally, Chapter 7 should provide some guidance to the many resources that are available to assist anyone concerned about employee benefits: books, periodicals, organizations, outside consultants, and so on.

1
AN INTRODUCTION TO EMPLOYEE BENEFITS

EMPLOYEE BENEFITS TODAY

Not too long ago things were pretty simple. Setting up a company's employee benefits program was rather cut and dried. You signed up with Blue Cross for a health insurance plan to cover your employees. You bought a group life insurance policy. You might make an annual contribution to some kind of pension plan. You might decide to offer a few other employee benefits that didn't cost very much or require much real attention from management. And, in any case, a "comp and benefits" manager in the personnel department usually took care of all the details.

But all this has changed. Employee benefits, like it or not, are now a major concern to anyone who runs a business. The acronyms and buzzwords are becoming commonplace in the business press and even, every so often, on the front pages of the daily newspapers: "skyrocketing" health costs, Section 401[k] plans, HMOs, ESOPs, PAYSOPs, defined contribution-plans, defined-benefit plans, plan termination, self-funding, coinsurance, ERISA, LTD, EAPs, AD&D, SPDs,

1

cafeteria plans, final average pay, ERTA, TEFRA, DEFRA, VEBAs, FSAs, SERPs, joint and survivor options, top-heavy plans, PBGC, PPOs, UCR charges, OASDHI, Social Security offsets, cliff vesting, SUB, and so on, and so on.

Don't laugh. A well-informed executive—or, in fact, anyone with even partial responsibility for a firm's employee benefits today—should be familiar with all of the above.

And, looming ever higher over the horizon, is the prospect of additional employee benefit taxation, which may, in years to come, present business executives with some of the toughest decisions of all.

The expense of a company's employee benefit program today amounts to a large percentage of its payroll. The exact figure, of course, varies considerably from company to company and depends, to a large extent, on exactly what you call a "benefit" and how you calculate its real cost. However, the cost of even a bare-bones benefits program will almost surely be about 10 percent of payroll. And, when the cost of sick leave and other time not worked is included, the minimum cost of benefits will be equal to at least a quarter of a company's total expenditures for wages. For those companies with lavish arrangements, the costs can approach as much as 40 or 50 percent of payroll. It should come as no surprise, then, to find that major decisions about employee benefits must often be made at the very highest levels of any company's management.

Management of employee benefits has now become so all-encompassing that almost any executive who has responsibility for handling people—or, to use the now-popular teminology, managing human resources—must know a lot about employee benefits.

One word of definition: as the long list of topics covered in Chapter 2 demonstrates, a "benefit" can be just about anything that an employee receives from his or her company *except* cash wages. Most benefits are paid for, at least in part, by the employer. Some are relatively cheap, or even cost-free; others are quite costly—and getting more so every day. Some are required by law; most are not. And some employee benefits are favorably treated by the tax laws, while others are not (a distinction that may become increasingly blurred in the future).

WHY BOTHER WITH BENEFITS?

That's a question that is being asked within many a company. With all the complications, expense, and general headaches involved, wouldn't it be simpler just to forget about benefits? Why not simply pay people a lot more in straight wages and let them take care of everything for themselves?

This might be a tempting solution, but one that, in today's business climate, would be most difficult...and extraordinary. It could be possible, at least in theory, in a few very special cases—for example, a small, newly organized high-technology company in which everyone received extremely high wages, stock options, and other lucrative compensation. Also almost all employees would have to be young and single or have spouses who held secure, well-paying jobs (and good benefits programs).

Such a company, needless to say, is a rarity. (And even it would be well advised not to eliminate such benefits as vacations and sick leave.) Everyone else is compelled to give careful consideration to employee benefits as an essential element of each worker's total compensation. In fact, that's exactly how benefits are usually thought of today—as a basic segment of what a person is paid, not simply as "fringes" to be added grudgingly onto wages almost as an afterthought.

Companies' employee benefits programs have grown and become more complicated over the years. No universal pattern has emerged; each company has its own reasons for ending up with the special combination of benefits that it now offers. If it were asked why it had done so, the answers might include:

"It's required by law"

Some employee benefits, such as Social Security, workers' compensation, and, in most states, unemployment insurance are legally required. And these are expensive enough. However, that's about as far as the law goes in the United States. In striking contrast to the situation in many European countries, American companies have no legal obligation to provide their employees with anything else—even a paid vacation.

However, there's no guarantee that this will always be the case. One good reason for private industry to voluntarily provide benefits could be to reduce any pressure for future government-required programs that would fill the void.

"We owe it to our employees"

Many companies truly believe that it's part of their duty as good citizens to protect their employees against possible perils. In fact, it once was frequently heard that a company's benefits program was designed to protect people against four disasters: death, disability, ill health, and retirement. (Actually, "retirement" never quite fit into this foursome, but it made a nice, neat concept—something that could be cleverly illustrated in a benefits booklet.)

While a good employee benefits program today does much more than this, of course, its rationale may not have changed. Most business executives do feel a genuine responsibility for the well-being of their employees and their employees' families.

It's difficult to disagree with this sentiment, paternalistic as it may be. However, it does create one potential problem: An executive who sets up a nobly intended benefits program can fall into the trap of believing that his or her own special needs and interests are exactly what everyone else should have, too...a "Papa knows best" attitude. Thus, someone who is very much concerned about having, say, a generous pension plan, a convenient vehicle for investing pretax dollars, and a healthy amount of life insurance can honestly believe that these are the most important objectives of the company's benefits program. But, in truth, many younger employees might have little interest in *any* of these benefits. Instead, they might find simpler things—a good tuition-refund program or an extra week of vacation—much more attractive.

"It's a tax-effective way to compensate people"
This is certainly a good economic justification for a generous employee benefits program. As we shall explain in Chapter 2, the costs of many benefits plans are (under current law, at least) tax-deductible business expenses for an employer who provides them. And many of these benefits, such as health insurance or basic life insurance premiums, are considered to be nontaxable income for employees; others, such as payments received from most pension and profit-sharing plans, are tax-*deferred* income.

Recently pressure has increased for the government to start taxing some of these traditionally untaxed benefits; this is an important issue that cannot be easily dismissed or resolved. (In Chapter 4, we shall discuss the issue of benefits taxation at some length.)

"Benefits help us attract and keep good people"
At one time this was a more valid argument for an innovative benefits program than it is today. But now, especially in areas where almost every large company offers at least a core of basic benefits, it's much less likely to hold true. A poor benefits program will certainly be unattractive, but only when a program is an unusually good one will it get very much positive attention.

And of course, some especially generous benefits still do attract people to certain jobs. Four-month vacations may make up for the low pay scales of college teaching, and free tickets to faraway places still lure people to the airlines.

But, even though people may not sign up with a company because of its wonderful pension plan—or suddenly leave to join another company that has better medical insurance—this doesn't mean you can always ignore the next reason.

"We have to keep up with the competition"

This has always been the easiest justification for adding on some new benefit. If most of the large companies in a small city are offering dental plans, it's difficult not to do likewise—especially if you're in a tight labor situation.

Highly visible and often-used plans, such as those covering dental and vision care or those matching employees' savings contributions, are particularly susceptible to competitive pressure like this. It's much harder for prospective employees to analyze and compare two companies' pension programs or long-term disability plans.

In fact, the whole process of comparing oneself to others in the same geographic area or the same industry sometimes can get out of hand. A company can go to great lengths, often with the aid of elaborate statistical surveys and extremely detailed comparisons, to determine exactly how its benefits program stacks up against those of the competition. This analysis might be an interesting intellectual exercise, but it is probably not worth the trouble or expense. Who *really* cares if one company's retirement plan pays 42.5 percent of final pay to a 30-year employee and another company's pays 43.7 percent? (And there's not very much either 30-year employee can do about it at this date, certainly.)

After all, no two companies have exactly the same human resources objectives or the same mix of employees. It would seem much more important for each of them to design the benefits program that was the best for its own people—not to worry constantly about what the competition is doing.

"Benefits are good for morale"

Yes, they are. But, unfortunately, most employees have come to accept employee benefits as a matter of course. It's asking a lot to hope that improving benefits will do much to help productivity or decrease turnover. These are usually deep-rooted problems not susceptible to quick fixes. Some people have even tried to find a way to measure the "return on investment" for benefits in terms of better employee performance—a difficult task that is doomed to disappointment.

In fact, the real danger comes from the other direction: Reducing benefits—or even appearing to do so—can have a negative effect on morale or productivity. A company will surely feel the backlash if it ever should attempt to eliminate—or even slightly reduce—a long-established benefit.

"The unions are behind it"
This works both ways. Labor unions have often negotiated such immediately recognizable benefits as dental insurance, prescription-drug plans, and employer-pays-all health insurance into a contract. And, in times of economic stress, they have fought mightily to retain these hard-won benefits—sometimes even in preference to cash wages.

On the other hand, these same benefits have appeared in nonunion companies when employers became convinced that they had better provide a certain benefit, or a union will dangle some new benefit as a glittering promise in an organizational campaign.

"Benefits provide economies of scale"
This can be a good reason why a company might offer some kinds of benefits, such as supplemental life insurance, simply to make it possible for employees to get lower group rates—even if the company doesn't contribute any of its own money. The mathematics of group insurance permits members of a group to pay less for most kinds of coverage than they would as individuals. This may be obvious, but it can come as a nasty shock when someone leaves a company and converts group health insurance to an individual plan.

To Sum Up
We've now examined eight possible answers to the question we posed earlier: Why bother with having employee benefits? Any one company's reasoning will doubtless include elements

of several of these answers—perhaps all eight. But, whatever the combination of answers may be, it's really the most important question to decide before going any further. For if you don't know exactly why you are worrying about benefits in the first place, you really can't make intelligent decisions about individual benefit plans themselves.

NEEDS VS. REWARDS

In addition to the specific reasons for setting up an employee benefits program, there is something that might be thought of as a company's general philosophy: When you really get down to basics, are benefits to be thought of as ways to fulfill employee *needs*, or are they, on the other hand, *rewards* to compensate employees for services rendered?

Benefits for needs
Looking at employee benefits from this first point of view, a company would consider the problems that its employees are most likely to face—and how an employee benefits program could help. This kind of thinking would place most emphasis on the benefits that protect against potential disasters: life insurance, major medical, long-term disability coverage, and the like. And the retirement program would be designed to provide employees with a lifetime income that, with Social Security, would be enough to supply their basic needs. There might, of course, be other elements in a company's program, but they would be subordinate to those plans that filled basic human needs.

This is the traditional approach to benefits planning, and the one that many companies still take. And it's not necessarily as hard-nosed as it may sound. Although the company may supply only the basic core of benefits, it might very well compensate its employees quite handsomely. The feeling would be that, in this way, employees will be able to choose the benefits they most need—and pay for them out of their own well-lined pockets.

Benefits as rewards

A different philosophical approach is to look at benefits primarily as a form of compensation. With this in mind, a company's benefits program will start off by protecting employees against disaster, but will move on from there. It will place greater emphasis on those extra benefit plans that, although not essential, will be very much appreciated by employees. These might include: taking a more liberal approach to vacations and other time off; offering supplementary health plans, such as dental and vision care; and placing more emphasis on profit-sharing, savings, and other capital-accumulation plans.

When this approach is taken, benefits can be allocated, to some extent, as appropriate rewards to those employees who most deserve them. An employee's benefits are viewed as essential parts of the total compensation package. Thus, a company may not feel constrained to limit these earned benefits—even if tax laws should view them with less favor. In addition, a fairly lavish benefits program can be used for its public relations value, in enhancing the company's image as a good provider and in attracting recruits.

Benefits and the bottom line

A company, then, can be influenced by two general attitudes toward employee benefits. Call them what you will: needs vs. rewards; protection vs. compensation; realistic vs. paternalistic; conservative vs. liberal; hard-hearted vs. soft-headed. The two philosophies, of course, are not mutually exclusive. Very few companies will be totally in one camp or the other. Most benefits programs will end up with elements of each of the two philosophies. And, since all companies are different, that's not at all surprising.

For some companies, however, the fast-rising cost of benefits may force a quite different decision. Economics may prevail over philosophy. Whichever approach a company might like to take—all else being equal—it may be *most* influenced by one of its own basic needs: financial survival. With this as an overriding consideration, its approach to employee benefits may be simplest of all: How much can we afford to spend on them? And here, more than ever, it would indeed seem foolish to spend a lot of money on across-the-board benefit plans that many employees don't need and will never use.

A LITTLE BENEFITS HISTORY

As we shall mention in Chapter 2, when we discuss the various kinds of benefits plans, many of them have an impressive history. Long before today's elaborate and generous employee benefits programs became almost universal, some progressive companies decided, for one reason or another, to protect their employees against life's hazards. However, this was usually done in a hit-or-miss fashion. And the Great Depression of the early 1930s took a heavy toll on the embryonic employee benefits plans movement in private industry.

Then, in 1935, Social Security—the country's first national government-operated benefit plan—came into existence. But, in contrast to what happened in other countries, government-sponsored programs did not proliferate here after Social Security. In the United States, the task of providing workers with shields against many of life's dangers fell to the private sector. (The very words "social security" in most Western nations today imply a much more all-encompassing program than ours—one that may also include unemployment compensation, maternity benefits, and universal health insurance.)

By an accident of history, World War II exerted a strong influence on the course that employee benefits was to take in this country. During the war, wage control laws prevented companies from granting pay increases to their employees. So they began to devise some ingenious substitutes that were perfectly legal: employee benefit plans. And, after the war, no one was about to give up what had been gained. Labor unions realized that benefits offered something more to negotiate for their members.

Ever since, the privately supported benefits movement has grown and prospered. For a time, not many people really understood what was happening. But now almost everyone is quite aware of the importance of employee benefits—and the federal government is giving them more attention than ever before.

A CHANGING POPULATION—AND HOW IT AFFECTS BENEFITS

When benefit plans were in their infancy, their provisions usually were designed with just one kind of employee in mind: a male breadwinner who stayed married to a woman who was content to be a full-time homemaker taking care of a growing family of children. And this man could usually look forward to spending the rest of his life working loyally for the same company.

Of course, even then, there were a great many workers who didn't fit this pattern. But little attention was paid to their special needs—perhaps because the people who devised benefits plans usually *did* fit the mold.

Today, no one has to be told that we live in a much different world. The demographics are different, and they must be carefully considered. Some of the important new considerations are:

- A work force that, in general, is older and better educated, with more minority-group representation, and, especially, with...
- A much greater number of women, many of whom are now moving up to executive positions.
- Smaller families, because of more than three decades of declining birthrates.
- More women who leave the work force only temporarily, to have children.
- A growing number of two-earner couples, each well paid, with or without children.

- More divorces and remarriages—and sometimes the obligation to support two sets of children.
- More single parents (usually women, but including a surprising number of men).
- But, at the same time, more "empty nesters" and other single-person households without dependents to care for.
- Improvements in medicine—and personal health awareness—that are resulting in greater life expectancy.
- But more interest in early retirement, too—so that the retired population is increasing in even greater numbers.
- More new and different job opportunities in a fast-changing economy, which leads to greater career flexibility and...
- Much less feeling of lifetime commitment to one company.

All these trends, in one way or another, have had a tremendous impact on the kind of employee benefits program that a company sets up. Benefit plans that date back to the days of the traditional one-earner-with-dependents-at-home family are no longer appropriate for today's potpourri of varied family arrangements.

But this doesn't mean that radical changes are necessarily in order. In most cases, a company's existing benefit programs can be adjusted to fit a variety of family needs. Each company must examine its own mix of employees. And that means what it is *right now*, not what it was when the benefit plans were originally established. Only then can the benefits package be retailored for this unique combination of people.

One of the best ways to do this, many companies are finding, is to accept the fact that it just isn't possible to devise an across-the-board benefits program that will best suit every employee's family today. Why not, then, allow employees to have some say in choosing their own benefits? That's the reasoning behind *flexible benefits*, which we discuss at length in Chapter 4.

SOME BASIC BENEFITS PRINCIPLES

1. There are many good reasons to have an employee benefit program; each company must decide which are most important.

2. A company can either supply just the basic core of benefits or, in addition, offer a broad array of supplemental plans—depending on its basic benefits philosophy...or what it can afford.

3. Workers today are far different from what they were when most conventional benefit plans were designed—and they know what they want.

4. The benefits that most appeal to company executives—including benefits managers—are not always the ones that are most popular with employees in general; a wise company will know its employees.

5. Each company's benefits program must be designed to fit its own particular mix of people; there are no easy, off-the-shelf solutions.

6. However, it's impossible to design a program that will be ideal for every employee in a company.

7. With benefits, you can be trapped by the past. A company that has a long history of providing a certain benefit will have great difficulty in eliminating this plan or making any drastic changes in its provisions.

8. Most benefits programs today do not discriminate among groups of employees, but there's really no reason why each and every employee should have exactly the same benefits.

9. Costs are obviously an extremely important consideration in all benefits planning, but the most attractive benefits are not necessarily those that cost the most.

10. The best solution, everything considered, may be for employees to have a share in deciding on their own benefits package, whenever possible.

So, keeping these principles in mind, let's now take a long, hard look at all the employee benefits that are available.

2
A GUIDE TO EMPLOYEE BENEFITS

In the following pages we shall discuss each of the employee benefits that are offered today to American workers. For convenience, these have been divided into ten groupings, which are presented approximately in the order of popularity—with the most commonly offered benefit plans being described (at some length) first, and the ones that are seen least often bringing up the rear.

The first seven sections of Chapter 2 are devoted to what might be called the "major" benefits. For these, we shall discuss the special provisions of each benefit and then bring up some important points that any company planning to offer this particular benefit should consider carefully.

These sections are:

- Time Off: Sick Pay/Short-Term Disability; Vacation; Holidays; Other Time Off
- Health Insurance, including an extended discussion of cost containment and health maintenance organizations
- Other Kinds of Health Protection: Dental Insurance; Vision Care; Prescription-Drug Plans; Physical Examinations; "Wellness" Programs; Employee Assistance Programs

- Life Insurance
- Long-Term Disability Insurance
- Pensions, with the emphasis on conventional defined-benefit plans
- Other Retirement and Capital-Accumulation Programs: Profit-Sharing Plans; Stock-Ownership Plans; Thrift and Savings Plans; Cash-or-Deferred Arrangements; Social Security; Preretirement Planning Programs

The final sections cover, more briefly, the many other special benefits that are offered today. We have divided these into three groups:

- Special Services: Child Care; Legal Services; Property and Liability Insurance; Tuition Reimbursement; Other Educational Assistance; Philanthropy
- Employment-Related Benefits: Government-Required Programs; Supplemental Unemployment Benefits; Relocation Assistance; Suggestion Plans; Commutation Assistance; Credit Unions, Stock Purchase Plans; Merchandise Discounts; Gifts; Subsidized Food Service; Health and Recreation Programs; Employee Clubs and Activities; Service Awards
- Benefits Primarily for Executives: Special Compensation Arrangements; Supplemental Retirement Plans; Stock Options; Financial Counseling; Executive Perquisites

TIME OFF

Providing employees with paid time off from work—for holidays, sick leave, and the like—may be the most popular and cost-effective benefit of them all. Yet, to some benefits executives, time off is held in such low regard that it isn't even considered a "benefit"—it's simply something that is built into the compensation structure. Booklets describing a company's employee benefits program may go into intimate detail about such eyeglazers as the accidental death or dismemberment clause or the joint and survivor option but barely mention the vacation schedule.

To many employees, however, paid time off is the one benefit they really appreciate—and one of the few that may even be important enough to influence a decision about whether to join one company or another. Can it be that senior executives, who can often set their own vacation schedules (or are workalcoholics who never take one), have forgotten how important that two or three weeks off can be to an ordinary employee?

In the new flexible benefits programs, in which employees can choose some of the benefits they receive, the popularity of vacation time has sometimes come as a rude shock. When offered a variety of benefits to select from, many employees—the younger ones in particular—will often pass up supplemental life insurance or a dental plan for an extra week of vacation.

Note: In addition to the kinds of time off we shall discuss in this section, many workers also, of course, receive the benefit of scheduled time off for lunch, rest periods, coffee breaks, washing up, and the like.

SICK PAY/SHORT-TERM DISABILITY

This is a benefit that, sooner or later, virtually every employee will make use of. Yet it's a benefit that can, if not controlled properly, lead to surprising amounts of ill feeling and resentment.

Having to provide pay—either full salary or part of it—to employees who call in sick is one of those necessary evils of running any sort of business. No one likes doing it, but one can hardly avoid the chore. Except for temporary hourly workers and the self-employed, almost everyone seems to deem it an inalienable right to be paid when he or she feels too sick to work.

HOW IT WORKS

Although being paid in this way is certainly a benefit in the technical sense, the whole question of sick pay should be simply a matter of establishing a personnel policy. Companies have two choices: (1) to set up a hard-and-fast written policy and stick to it, making no exceptions, or (2) to play it by ear, having no formal policy but treating each case of absence individually according to its own merits.

Under the first arrangement, fairness to all is guaranteed, at least superficially. But there's always the problem of the very unusual situation, when an exception to the standard policy seems eminently justifiable. And then, once you have made one exception, there surely will be more. So what has happened to the fixed policy?

Treating each case individually, on the other hand, means that each person's family and health situation is considered. But this policy presents a new set of problems. It requires a lot of administrative and supervisory work and, unfortunately, is all too subject to abuse—human nature being what it is. Some people will call in sick two or three times every month with real, fancied, or nonexistent complaints; others will drag in their aching bodies until they must almost be physically forced to go home to bed.

Salary continuation

This is the simplest way to handle short-term illnesses—and what's usually done if there is no formal sick-pay policy. It means simply to continue paying regular salary to people who can't work because of sickness. And, if absences become so frequent that there seems no other solution to the problem, the employee can be warned, put on probation, or, eventually, terminated.

With a formal salary-continuation policy, the element of uncertainty disappears. Each employee is allotted a certain number of sick-leave days in a specified period, usually a year. It may be possible to carry unused days over from year to year, or the policy may simply be "use it or lose it." The number of days per year may increase with length of service, or perhaps with employment status.

In any case, the real costs of short-term disability shouldn't be exaggerated—unless, of course, a temporary substitute must actually be hired to fill in for an absent employee. Very often, the job will be covered for a day or two by co-workers—or work will simply pile up until the absentee returns. This affects overall productivity, obviously, but it's something that isn't unexpected—and a realistic company will plan in advance for a certain amount of unavoidable absenteeism during the course of a year.

All this sounds fine in theory, of course, but a company must always decide when it must stand firmly on its formal policy...and when to make an exception. What do you do, for example, if a valuable employee who is only entitled to 10 days of sick leave is seriously ill for three weeks? Do you *really* want abruptly to stop paying a full salary check after the second week?

Short-term disability plans

Many companies have formal plans that set a fixed schedule of payments to employees who can't work because of illness or accident. In some states, in fact, the law requires that employers provide this kind of "temporary disability insurance" (see below).

These plans are deliberately designed to be in effect for a limited period: usually from when an employee stops receiving regular paychecks until he or she becomes eligible for the company's long-term disability plan or disability insurance under Social Security (whichever comes first).

Short-term coverage of this kind can be handled by an insurance company, which can provide outside review of claims. But, since this is, by definition, *short-term* insurance, the total liability will never be very large, and an increasing number of firms now are self-insuring this kind of coverage. In any case, premiums are almost always paid entirely by the employer.

The guidelines on how much an employee receives while on short-term disability are similar to those for long-term disability insurance (see below). Payment may be a percentage of gross salary, often one-half or two-thirds, or, less often, a flat dollar amount. And it's very common for the amount of short-term disability pay to be based on length of service, according to a sliding scale.

In explaining a company's policy on short-term disability absences to employees, salary continuation and disability insurance are often, for convenience, lumped together. Such as: "With service of less than one year, you are eligible for sick pay of one week at full pay plus two weeks at half pay...after 10 years' service you are eligible for 13 weeks at full pay plus 13 weeks at half pay...and so on."

As with long-term disability, overlapping coverage is a possible problem. For this reason, short-term plans almost always are limited to a stretch of 26 weeks at the very most, after which an employee usually is eligible for some other kind of disability payments, either through a long-term plan or from Social Security.

SOME THINGS TO CONSIDER ABOUT SHORT-TERM DISABILITY
What about pregnancy?
The law is very clear on this point. Under the Pregnancy Discrimination Act of 1978, if a company has a formal plan of any kind that covers disability, a woman who is absent because of pregnancy must be treated exactly like anyone who is absent because of accident or illness. She need only have her physician certify how long her condition—both before and after the birth of a child—prevents her from working. In other words, a short-term disability plan cannot have any special requirements—such as specifying a fixed number of weeks of paid absence—that apply only to cases of pregnancy.

What about the possibility of malingering?
In a perfect world, of course, this wouldn't be an issue. Nevertheless, any company must face the fact that some

employees will try to take advantage of a generous short-term disability plan. As a result, such controls as requiring medical proof that an absence is genuine are usually built in. Another solution is to have a waiting period of a few days before payments begin—often with retroactive pay for waiting-period days if the illness turns out to be serious. Of course, this kind of policy sometimes can backfire: If an employee knows that he or she won't be paid for an absence of only one or two days—but *will* be paid if the absence lasts three days or more—the number of three-day sicknesses, not surprisingly, will be unusually large.

Why not take a positive approach?
Sometimes a positive approach can be quite effective. A company can offer a special "wellness" bonus of some kind for employees with good attendance records. Or employees might be able to bank their unused sick days from year to year—until the time when they are really needed.

VACATION

This is undoubtedly a benefit that is extremely popular with employees, but, strangely, a benefit in which the United States lags far behind many other countries in generosity. Because of the almost universal interest in vacations, it is especially important that a company's vacation policy be clearly understood by everyone. And this policy, whether conservative or liberal, should be based on the reasons why vacations are being given in the first place.

Are they to provide employees with rest and relaxation away from the job, so that their productivity will increase when they return? Or to offer a relatively low-cost benefit that will appeal to prospective employees, particularly in a competitive environment? Or simply as the customary reward for a fixed period of service, which, like it or not, can't be avoided?

VACATION POLICY GUIDELINES

Vacation, over the years, has almost always been one benefit that is dependent upon length of service alone. Most employees, in fact, won't see anything unusual if a newly hired middle manager gets only two weeks of vacation while his secretary, a long-time company employee, gets four weeks.

Of course, the amount of vacation *can* be based on other factors besides service. Executives above a certain level may be awarded additional weeks of vacation; sometimes this is a necessary inducement to lure a valuable person with built-up vacation credit away from another company. Extra weeks of vacation can also be used as an incentive bonus for extraordinary performance, as compensation for an unusual amount of unpaid overtime, or to give special recognition in anniversary years. (One innovation that never really caught on was to provide an extended "sabbatical" every five years to long-term employees, which the United Steelworkers negotiated some time ago.)

On the surface, setting up a company's vacation policy seems rather straightforward. But, unless every possible source of ambiguity is eliminated at the very beginning, vacation can be the source of many unforeseen problems, misinterpretations, and ill feeling.

Here are some of the simple, but potentially controversial, points that a vacation policy should make very clear:

- Exactly how many days (if any) of vacation does someone who starts work in the middle of a year get—and when can these be taken?
- Can vacation days be carried over until the next year? The year after?
- Can vacation be taken a day at a time, or must it be on a weekly basis only?
- Must a vacation be in certain months only—or at any time during the year?
- What happens if there is a holiday during your vacation? What if you get sick?

- And what about people who can't take a scheduled vacation because of an unexpected work load?
- Is it possible to take extra unpaid days on top of a regular paid vacation?
- Is someone who leaves voluntarily entitled to pay in lieu of vacation days not yet taken?

SOME THINGS TO CONSIDER ABOUT VACATION

Why not give everyone the same vacation?
In some industries, it is customary to substitute a general plant shutdown for individual vacation time. (In countries like France, of course, everyone simply takes the month of August off!) This avoids many of the possible problems, and works out well for everyone...except, of course, for those whose vacation time doesn't coincide with that of the rest of their family. For most American firms that must remain in continuous operation for 52 weeks a year, however, a company-wide standard vacation isn't very practical—although closing the entire operation early on Friday afternoons in summer is a growing practice.

How much does vacation cost?
This is a trickier question than it might seem. When they talk about the costs of benefits—especially in labor union negotiations—companies love to say how much they spend on vacations. But the true cost is never that simple to calculate. You can't just add up the payroll and multiply it by the number of vacation days taken. In those businesses where substitutes must be hired or extra overtime paid when some employees are on vacation, this may be reasonably accurate arithmetic. But in a company where co-workers simply cover for a vacationing employee, or where employees must make up the work themselves either before or after their vacation, the true cost may actually be close to zero.

HOLIDAYS

Holidays are usually taken more or less for granted. Since they occur at irregular intervals and there are so many variations in observance, they have only minor impact as a benefit. Holidays simply exist as parts of the yearly calendar. Only when a company is very much out of line with the practices of similar institutions in its immediate vicinity does anyone even notice. And very little is gained by giving employees a holiday that other firms in the area don't observe.

The "Big Six"
The United States has only six truly national holidays—fewer than many other Western countries. Three of them (Memorial Day, Labor Day, and Thanksgiving) occur on the same day of the week every year, and thus exist as predictable features of the annual calendar. (The only question: What to do about the day after Thanksgiving?)

The others (New Year's Day, Independence Day, and Christmas) float from day to day in the week and can occasionally present minor, but easily anticipated, problems. When one of these three falls on Sunday, it has become a regular custom to celebrate it on Monday, but if it falls on Saturday there is no consistent national practice to fall back on. Employees can be given the preceding Friday off, the following Monday, a compensatory day at some other time in the year, or nothing at all (which, obviously, will make no one particularly happy).

Minor holidays
We now come to the other possibilities: the birthdays of Washington, Lincoln, and Martin Luther King; Good Friday; Columbus Day; Election Day; and Veterans' Day, plus a number of regional holidays, such as Patriots Day in Massachusetts. All you can really do is follow local practice as best you can.

For the sake of consistency, a company with operations in many states might be tempted to set a single holiday policy for the entire country; this could be more trouble than it's worth. If a local holiday in one state means that the banks, schools, post offices, and most of the firms you do business with are all closed, it doesn't make much sense for you to keep your local office open, despite the national company policy. You won't get much accomplished and you'll create a lot of unnecessary resentment among your employees.

When minor holidays occur on weekends, the practice of awarding an alternative day off is not so universal. In this case, employees may simply be out of luck.

However a company decides to handle its holiday schedule, it's important to give employees adequate advance notice of any contemplated changes from one year to the next. Management won't win many friends by suddenly announcing on October 1 that—guess what?—we aren't going to celebrate Columbus Day this year, even though we did so last year.

SOME THINGS TO CONSIDER ABOUT HOLIDAYS
Do "floating" holidays make sense?
In any given year, there will inevitably be quirks in the calendar that can be potential problems—such as when a major holiday falls on Tuesday or Thursday, or, as we mentioned, when a minor holiday falls on Saturday. To allow for these times, many companies have adopted a regular policy of adding one or two floating holidays to the annual schedule and assigning them to an appropriate date on a year-to-year basis.

What about religious holidays?
In most cases, these can be easily provided for if a company adopts a relatively liberal policy regarding personal time. There's no need to arouse even the faint possibility of hurt feelings or resentment among employees of different religions.

How much do holidays cost?
Strictly speaking, nothing at all. Since their exact dates are known in advance, a year's work schedule can be established by building around these days, whenever they may occur. Even a business or service that is regularly open on holidays, and must pay employees extra, can discount this cost at the beginning of a year.

OTHER TIME OFF

Sickness, vacations, and holidays do not exhaust the possibilities for granting employees time away from the job. As with sick pay, a company really has two choices as to how it treats other kinds of paid time off. It can follow a strictly formal policy—exactly so many days off for this particular reason and nothing more—without exceptions. Or it can have a flexible policy of treating each situation individually as it comes along. With the first policy, there's the problem of not being able to handle the truly exceptional situation; with the second policy, there's the danger that employees may take advantage of the company's generosity. What any one company does probably will depend very much on its own employee relations.

VARIETIES OF PAID TIME OFF
Personal days
Almost every employee, at one time or another, will feel the need to take time off from work for some reason other than personal illness. Companies have begun to accept the inevitable. Granting a specified number of annual paid days off should take care of those unexpected events that don't fit into any special categories—but which, to a particular employee, can be matters of great importance. Personal days off can also be used, as mentioned above, for religious observances.

Jury duty

Various federal and state laws require that companies grant employees time off for jury duty if their names are picked. Although some people will do everything in their power to avoid serving (sometimes, regrettably, with their employers' connivance), most will eventually find themselves doing their civic duty. Companies are not required to pay their employees while they serve on a jury. But most do so—even if it's only to make up the difference between the jury fee and an employee's regular salary. It once was customary to ask employees to hand over the relatively small checks they receive for jury service, but this would seem to create more resentment than the minuscule cash return to the company might warrant. Occasionally, an employee may also be called to serve as a witness in a trial or some other legal proceeding; a company's jury duty policy should cover this rare event also.

Death in the family

Granting compassionate leave when there is a death in an employee's family is the long-standing practice of almost every company. The only questions seem to be how far the definition of "family" can be extended, and how many paid days off should be given. However, there is no conceivable way of judging how close anyone may have been to a particular relative, and setting up formal guidelines to regulate the allowable extent of grief is somewhat distasteful. This is one area where almost any company would be advised to treat each situation on a strictly individual basis.

Family illness/medical emergency

This is another instance where individual discretion must be used. And here, as elsewhere, a supervisor should exercise good judgment.

Military service

In years past, this was a major employee benefits concern. Today, however, with the relatively small number of people with military obligations, it should be no problem. A company may decide to pay employees full salary while they are on reserve duty, make up the difference between military pay and regular pay, or (if especially hard-nosed) ask them to use any required annual vacation for their military duty.

Marriage

Granting a fixed number of paid days off for an employee's wedding and honeymoon doesn't cost much and can win a lot of friends. And it's one benefit that's particularly welcome to younger employees.

Unpaid time off

In addition to what has been mentioned thus far, there may be times when some employees ask to take a leave of absence without pay. These could be for regular military duty, to continue one's education full time, to take up a temporary civic or political appointment, to care for an infant temporarily, or simply to go on an extended unpaid vacation. Except in the case of military service, there is no legal obligation for a company to hold open an employee's old job during this kind of absence—or, in fact, to offer any kind of reemployment. (This includes employees on maternity leave that extends beyond pregnancy disability—although laws in this case might well change in the future.) However, depending on the value of a particular employee, a company may well wish to arrange some kind of reemployment agreement in cases of this kind.

To Sum Up

- Although short-term disability can be an administrative headache, it is an often-used benefit that a company, realistically, must be prepared for. The total costs are usually not exorbitant, and a company has the option of setting up a formal policy or treating each occasion on an individual basis.
- Vacation is a universal benefit whose attractiveness to employees can easily be underestimated. An especially generous vacation policy thus can be an inexpensive sel-

ling point for a company—more so than many formal benefits plans.
- But vacation policy can become enmeshed in a number of minor but annoying disagreements, if its details are not firmly established and communicated.
- Holiday policies are only noticeable when a company *doesn't* keep up with common local observance, whatever it may be.
- Like it or not, employees will want to take time off for one good reason or another. Accepting this as inevitable and granting everyone a fixed number of personal days may help to head off minor but unpleasant problems.

HEALTH INSURANCE

The only formal employee benefit plan that many people think about as a "benefit"—even if the plan is never used—is the kind of medical and hospital insurance that their employer provides for them. Medical and hospital insurance differs from most of the other major benefits in one important aspect: It is current insurance—something that might be used at any moment. It isn't protection against some almost unthinkable disaster, like long-term disability or life insurance. Nor does it offer financial security for the far-off future, like a pension plan.

It's an extremely important benefit to almost all kinds of employees—young or old, married or single, male or female, high-paid or low-paid. Nevertheless, health insurance doesn't appeal to everyone; the big exception (and one whose numbers are growing continuously) is the employee whose husband or wife works at another company with a perfectly satisfactory medical plan that provides family protection.

Surprisingly enough—especially considering the tremendous costs of medical care today—employer-sponsored health insurance is a relatively new benefit in this country, which has had a long history of reliance on private medical care rather than national health insurance. Even Blue Cross itself—still almost the symbol of this benefit for many people—wasn't established until 1929, when it was first set up at Baylor University Hospital in Texas to cover a group of local schoolteachers. Although a scattering of other group plans were in existence in the early part of this century, medical insurance really didn't become important until World War II.

The first hospital and medical insurance plans were a far cry from what we know today. They usually offered a strictly limited menu of benefits, such as hospital care for a specified number of days and flat dollar amounts—or "indemnities"—for a list of surgical operations. Often there were no maternity benefits at all. (In those days an all-too-typical benefits manager—a lifelong bachelor, as it happened—once said that his company's plan would never cover childbirth because "that's *voluntary* and we only pay employees when they get sick or have an accident"!)

We live in a much different world today, of course. More than three-quarters of the American population is covered by health insurance of some kind—and there is Medicaid and free or low-cost public hospital services that provide, to some extent at least, emergency care for those who aren't covered. Only a small fraction of hospital costs today are paid for by individuals directly, which may be one reason why these costs are going up so rapidly.

HOW IT WORKS

Like all insurance, health protection works by spreading the risk. You charge the same premiums to a group of people, and those who stay healthy help pay the expenses of those who get sick. This holds true whatever arrangement you use—a private insurance company, one of the Blue Cross/Blue Shield groups, a health maintenance organization, or a company's own self-funded program. However, there are some quite important differences in how each of these kinds of insurance mechanism operates in actual practice:

Insurance companies
With an insurance company, you'll have an assortment of plans to choose from, and you'll have a big and fairly powerful company on your side in dealing with hospitals and doctors. But with a big company there also comes the danger of being lost in the shuffle of bureaucracy and paperwork—and the possibilities that people may have first to pay out their own money for medical charges, fill out some fairly complicated forms, and then wait to be reimbursed. And, of course, an insurance company has its own expenses, which someone must pay for.

Blue Cross/Blue Shield organizations
Using one of these long-established groups can make dealing with the hospitals easier because of their long-standing working arrangements (and possible discounts). But each of the "Blues" is an independent company covering its own geographical region; you're limited to the insurance plans offered by the one in your own area. So you may need to supplement a Blue Cross plan with a plan from an insurance company that provides more extensive major medical coverage, for instance. (Not too long ago, there were fundamental differences between the plans offered by insurance companies and the Blues—today they are getting more and more alike.)

Self-funded arrangements
A larger company can take on some of the risk by using its own finances to reimburse its employees' medical and hospital expenses. Thus, to some extent, the middleman is eliminated (although many companies still use an insurance company to handle the administrative chores of a health plan). The costs may be lower with this method—and a company's cash flow is certainly improved—but the risks of unexpectedly large ex-

penses are, of course, equally great. (This problem can be alleviated by using stop-loss insurance to guard against very large claims.) Another problem with self-funding is that employees who leave this kind of company plan usually can't convert their insurance as easily.

Health maintenance organizations (HMOs)
With an HMO, it's an entirely different ball game. As we explain later in the chapter, HMOs provide their members with paid-in-full medical care without the bother of filling out forms and applying for reimbursement. And they usually offer a number of special health maintenance services, such as physical exams and well-baby care, that aren't covered by the other plans. But you can only join an HMO that covers your own area, and your choice of doctors and hospitals will be quite limited.

WHAT TO LOOK FOR IN A HEALTH INSURANCE PLAN

Putting aside HMOs for the moment, let's look at some of the variables that you must take into consideration in examining any group plan for hospital and medical insurance. Here are the ways in which plans can differ from one another:

Who's covered by the plan?
Employees only or their family members as well? And in the latter (and much more common) case, just what family members will be eligible? Will the plan also be available to retirees? Disabled employees? Survivors of former employees after these employees die? Should part-time or temporary employees be covered, too? Can new employees join the plan on their first day of work—or should there be a waiting period?

Of course, every company will have its own feelings about these seemingly minor questions of eligibility, but these are decisions that must be made and incorporated into the plan at the very beginning. It's difficult to change the rules once the game has started. And it may be even harder to explain to a valued employee that, while her 19-year-old daughter won't be covered after she gets married, her 21-year-old son will be, since he's a full-time student.

Who pays for it?
This is a more fundamental question. Should the company take care of everything? Or, should employees pay the full premium? Or, much the most common solution today, should both the company and its employees share the costs? And, in this case, just how should these costs be split?

Health-insurance plans that are entirely company paid are getting very rare. Those that still remain are either the result of hard-fought labor negotiations or provide such modest benefits that the company doesn't have the nerve to ask its employees to share the cost. On the other hand, it would be a very tough-minded—or financially shaky—company of any size today that would ask its employees to foot the entire health-insurance bill. In small companies, of course, health insurance—if it's available at all—is much more likely to be paid for entirely by employees. Their only savings is the chance to take advantage of the insurance company's group rates.

Cost sharing can take several forms. A common practice is for the company to pay for its employees' own insurance but ask them to pay part or all of the extra charges for other family members. This does two things—it helps prevent needless duplicate coverage if people in their family are covered by other plans, and it deflects the complaint that a company is doing more for married employees than it is for single people.

Another solution is to split each increase in the insurance premium between company and employee according to a fixed ratio—such as 80 percent by the employer, 20 percent by the employee. This will make employees fully aware of each cost increase—small as it may be. Or the company may absorb all increases in premium rates as they come along, and only pass along some of the extra cost to employees every couple of years. While this is more generous, it only delays the inevitable bad news—which may be more difficult to communicate.

How are costs shared?
In early health-insurance plans, payments were usually always made on a "first dollar" basis. The plan paid the full cost of a medical service...but only up to a certain fixed amount. Above that, the patient had to pay anything else. This system worked fairly well when medical costs were reasonably low. But, as they began to rise sharply, the indemnity-schedule arrangement meant that almost all medical cost increases were passed on to employees.

To prevent this from happening, two other means of sharing costs began to appear more frequently: *deductibles* and *coinsurance*. These help share all costs—including the almost-inevitable increases—between employer and employees.

There's one complication, however: What happens when two family members, such as a husband and wife, each are covered by their own medical plans, and both have dependents' coverage? Suppose their child goes to the hospital, and each parent applies for repayment of 80 percent of the bills. Wouldn't they end up with a lot more reimbursement than they had actually paid out?

To prevent this, *coordination of benefits* (COB) clauses appear in almost all medical plans, restricting the total repayments from more than one plan to 100 percent of actual medical expenses. Thus, in this case, under recently announced COB rules, the plan of the parent whose birthday was earliest in the year would pay 80 percent; the other parent's plan would pay 20 percent.

What are the deductibles?
Under most health-insurance plans today, an employee pays a fixed deductible—usually once a year for each person covered (often with a maximum deductible for one family)—and the plan takes over after that. Deductibles, although never popular, at least are quite familiar and more-or-less

acceptable because of their common use elsewhere, such as in automobile insurance. There are some other advantages: They eliminate a lot of small claims (and their costly paperwork), and they may persuade employees—who must pay for the first dollars of medical expenses—not to incur unnecessary small charges for minor aches and pains.

Deductibles also offer a simple means of increasing the percentage of the costs of health care paid by employees, if a company wishes to do so (and many companies today are seeking to do exactly that). Raising the individual annual deductible, say, from $100 a person to $200 is easy to put into effect and simple to explain. (Although employees will never be happy to hear the announcement.)

Deductibles can present other problems to employees. It simply may be too much trouble to submit a series of small claims, even though these eventually will add up to more than the annual deductible, which means that employees can lose out on small repayments to which they are entitled. And, much more important, not seeing a doctor for a seemingly minor complaint may not be so wise if this "minor" problem actually is an early symptom of something much more serious (and expensive) in the long run.

Is there coinsurance?

Another common cost-sharing technique that is becoming quite familiar to health insurance users is coinsurance or copayment. Here the costs are split across the board. The plan pays a fixed percentage—50, 60, 70, 75, 80, or 90 percent—and the patient is responsible for the balance. (More often than not, the plan pays 80 percent.) This cost-splitting begins after the deductible, if there is one, is taken care of.

Even more than a deductible, coinsurance makes the user very much aware of how fast medical costs can pile up. Perhaps too much so, especially for people of limited means. Paying 20 percent may not sound so alarming, until this becomes 20 percent of a bill of several thousand dollars.

What are the out-of-pocket limits?
An increasingly common solution, therefore, has been to have some out-of-pocket or "stop-loss" provision that puts a limit on the total amount an employee must pay out for his or her share of the payments. This can be a fixed sum, such as $1,000 or $2,500, or a percentage of annual salary. In either case, this amount is the most that an employee has to pay out of his or her own funds. When expenses reach this ceiling, the coinsurance obligation ends, and the plan pays any additional bills in full.

This is a very important concept, but, for some reason, one that is often not very well communicated. All too many employees, faced with a serious family illness, begin to panic at the idea of paying 20 percent of an endless parade of bills—without realizing that it won't be as bad as all that.

What is the maximum coverage?
Something that gets much more publicity, but is actually much less important—is the plan's maximum coverage. This can be a quite impressive figure—$250,000, $500,000, $1,000,000, or even no limit at all. In truth, this limit is often meaningless, since the chances of any one person's bills ever reaching the plan's maximum are very slim.

However, increasing a plan's maximum actually costs very little, and a cynic might say that this is a good thing to do when a company wants to sugarcoat the announcement of something else—such as increasing the deductible—that will cost employees real money.

What is the general type of plan?
Sometimes, this can be the most confusing variable of all. It's often quite difficult to give a precise description of the kind of health insurance a company has in effect. As the industry has expanded, different forms of insurance have come into popularity. There are basic plans... supplemental plans... major medical plans... comprehensive plans... wraparound plans. All of these have specific meanings to the insurance in-

dustry, but they can be very confusing to the average employer—and certainly to the average worker.

The problem is even worse when, over the years, a company has accumulated its health-insurance coverage by starting off with one plan, and then added on another—and then perhaps a third—entirely separate plan. And, as this is happening, two or three entirely different insurance carriers may get into the act.

Actually, many of the complications are inherited from the time when hospital services and medical-surgical services were viewed as two separate and distinct benefits. (Even Blue Cross and Blue Shield started off as two different programs.) In recent years, however, the differences between them have become increasingly blurred. Whatever may be the origin of a complicated health-insurance program, it can be most confusing to anyone trying to use the plans—especially if hospital expenses are covered by one plan, doctor's bills by another (with a different insurance company), and prescription drugs by still a third kind of coverage. Often it's the employee who must figure out which of an assortment of company plans happens to cover his or her ailment—and then fill out two or even three separate forms. And the danger lurks of guessing wrong, filling out the wrong form, and waiting a long time to be reimbursed properly.

What's covered?

The specific charges covered by any one plan also can be difficult for a layman to figure out. Hospital plans—whether they pay in full or include a copayment or deductible—almost always cover the cost of a semiprivate room and board plus the usual associated charges such as nursing, routine tests, supplies, and the like (which often add up to an impressive sum on the final bill). And they specifically do not include personal expenses such as newspapers, telephone, or television rental.

From that point on, the variety in types of coverage is almost endless. Surgical bills, anesthesia charges, visits by a doctor in the hospital, X-rays, emergency-room treatment, intensive care, private nurses, ambulance service, blood transfusions, oxygen, casts and splints, and all the other possible expenses can be paid for (or *not* paid for) in a variety of ways. Only by reading the fine print can anyone *really* be sure what is and what isn't covered by a company's health-insurance plan...or plans.

Are there special exceptions?
Most plans also have some things that get entirely different treatment. One of these is mental illness. There usually is a different scale of payments for the various kinds of treatment for a mental disorder, often with a higher coinsurance percentage and a separate annual maximum. Most plans also have special provisions for private room charges, treatment in a nursing home, home health care, and other nonroutine expenses.

What are the exclusions?
Finally, it's important to know exactly what a health-insurance plan *doesn't* cover. Regular checkups for healthy children, physical exams, vision tests, cosmetic surgery, and the like are not included under most health-insurance plans. Nevertheless, some employees are inevitably going to run up medical expenses for things like these—and be very disappointed when they get the bad news.

To Sum Up:
Hospital and medical plans are seldom simple. Many variables exist in who is covered, who pays, how the payment is shared, what charges are and aren't covered, what limits are set, and all the rest. The essential reason for these variations is that many companies' health-insurance programs have simply evolved and been added to over the years; what finally results is often quite confusing to everyone.

COST CONTAINMENT
Since so much attention has been focused on health-care cost containment in recent years (with very good reason), we must

give it special attention here, even though, to some small extent at least, medical inflation has begun to slacken and hospital use is actually declining.

Unfortunately, some aspects of the problem—such as the increasing use of very costly new medical technology, the gradual aging of the population, and the alarming rise in malpractice awards by juries—are extremely difficult, if not impossible, to control. In the more manageable areas of health care, however, suggested remedies seem to crop up almost daily.

Possible solutions—and their drawbacks

Talking about cutting costs is always much easier than actually accomplishing anything. Some ideas come to the surface immediately: Why not make employees pay for more of their health insurance premiums? Why not increase deductibles or coinsurance...or both? Obviously, these will lower the costs of any company's health-insurance plan—at least temporarily. But they really aren't ways of cutting costs; they simply are means of shifting the cost—in this case, from the company to its employees. This may, in fact, be something that a company feels to be long overdue—but it's no way to control the *total* national health bill.

One argument in favor of shifting more of the costs to employees is that when someone else pays all the bills, people aren't too concerned with how large they are. But, if users must pay a share out of their own pocket, they'll become "wiser consumers" of medical care. However, this often is easier said than done; a person who needs medical attention doesn't always have the chance to shop around for the best deal.

A few employees, it must be admitted, actually may be getting more of a break on costs than they deserve—to the detriment of the system as a whole. Regrettably, there will be some people who submit fraudulent claims or apply for duplicate reimbursement, such as through both their own company's plan and their spouse's plan at the same time. So it's usually worthwhile for a company to pay more attention to administrative details and, if appropriate, spend money on computerized claim controls and an efficient coordination of benefits system to reduce duplicate claims.

And, of course, insurance companies make mistakes, too. Independent auditing of their bills usually pays dividends. In fact, some companies are making it worthwhile for employees to audit their own bills, by giving them a share of any money refunded in correcting legitimate overcharges they have discovered.

Another general approach to cost cutting is to substitute newer and lower-priced alternatives for familiar, and more expensive, medical-care practices whenever possible:

- Preadmission testing is cheaper than tests given while you take up a hospital bed.
- Requiring a doctor to "precertify" a surgical operation may keep its costs from increasing unexpectedly.
- Surgery in the outpatient department of a hospital, in a doctor's office, or at one of the new free-standing surgical centers costs less than the same procedure in a hospital's operating room.
- Patient care in a skilled nursing facility, a hospice, or at home is less expensive than the daily room charges at a full-fledged hospital.
- It doesn't make much sense to be admitted to a hospital over the weekend when nothing will get started until Monday.

Unfortunately, most of these well-intended efforts have not yet produced the hoped-for results. And, unfortunately, it is extremely difficult to measure what may be saved by any of these cost-cutting measures in actual dollars and cents. A more fundamental problem is that people tend to put themselves in the hands of their doctors when they are sick, and it's hard to contradict the doctor's orders—much as one might like to. (Most people, after all, would rather not go to the hospital in the first place.)

Even less popular with the medical profession are some

other often-proposed ways of cutting costs. For one thing, there's no foolproof way of putting pressure on a doctor whose charges exceed the established amounts that are "usual, customary, and reasonable."

Setting fixed payments for each *diagnosis-related group* (DRG) of illnesses is another current movement, which is gradually becoming required under Medicare. This system sets a standard amount of repayment for a specific ailment, no matter how many days a patient stays in a hospital. The DRG system might work in a government-controlled program, but it's much too early to tell if it would be successful with non-Medicare patients. In any case, two dangers are readily apparent: Fixed payments for Medicare patients might eventually shift extra costs to private patients, and the system could offer too strong an incentive for releasing a patient from the hospital prematurely.

Another cost-cutting system—something that a number of insurance companies have been pushing rather strongly—is mandatory *second opinions* for some common elective surgical procedures, such as hysterectomy, prostate removal, and operations on the knee. At first glance, this sounds good. When a second surgeon reviews the first one's recommendation, there may be a disagreement, and often this means that the surgery isn't performed. Or, if the employee chooses to go ahead with the surgery, the plan may pay a smaller share of the cost. Thus, at least in theory, thousands of dollars in surgical expenses are saved.

However, there remain a couple of nagging questions: Can we be sure that the second opinion (the one against an immediate operation) is *always* the correct one? And, if it isn't, this could mean that surgery is simply postponed until some later time, when additional complications may have arisen. This makes it difficult to obtain accurate figures on the true savings—over the long term—from second surgical opinions. Nevertheless, "second surgical" is becoming very popular. In some cases, employees now receive sharply reduced repayments if they fail to get a second opinion when their plan requires it.

A quite different approach to lowering overall medical costs has been to organize *coalitions* of employers. Through the joint efforts of a group of companies, direct pressure is brought to bear on the local medical community to keep prices under a fairly tight rein.

Working from the other direction is a rapidly growing movement in which groups of physicians and hospitals join together into various kinds of *preferred provider organizations* (PPOs), which usually contract to offer fixed discounted prices and better utilization review in return for rapid bill payment.

Although both employer coalitions and PPOs may very well achieve cost savings for the companies that participate, it is questionable whether the employees will always be as happy with a PPO's services as the company is with its prices. And, in fact, these may represent another, more subtle kind of cost shifting, wherein lower prices for a hospital's large and well-organized customers will simply be balanced off by *higher* prices to others who are smaller or less well organized. And there's also the danger that PPOs that fix prices may be accused of violating the antitrust laws.

Despite what's been said on these pages, there *is* hope. Although some of these suggested ways of cutting costs may have been oversold by their advocates, most of them will save *some* money, at least. And the jury is still out on many of them.

Cost-containment communications

In Chapter 6 we point out how effective employee communication can contribute to the success of almost any benefits objective. And containing the rising costs of health care is no exception. However, in seeking employees' cooperation in this effort, here are some points to keep in mind:

- Despite all the publicity, many employees may still be unaware of the dramatic rise in medical costs—especially if these have not yet affected them personally.
- Painting things much worse than they really are won't help;

horror stories like the claim that "General Motors spends more on medical insurance than it does on steel," for instance, have turned out to be gross exaggerations. (And certainly don't imply that's all their fault!)
- Don't be surprised if employees react strongly to anything that even *seems* to be a reduction in their medical coverage.
- Don't try to fool people; if employees must begin to pay more, tell them so straight out. (If the alternative is reduced benefits, they may not object so much as you might expect.)
- Employees often don't realize that their plan is self-funded, especially if it is being administered by a third party. They may be more sympathetic if they clearly recognize that increasing costs are being paid by their own company, not some giant insurance company.
- Many people are reluctant to second-guess their doctors; they won't enjoy mentioning a second opinion or asking to leave a hospital earlier.
- It's all very well to encourage people to shop around for the lowest-priced medical care; in real life this is often very difficult to do. But companies can help by gathering and communicating whatever data they can unearth about comparative prices.

Finally, let's examine two ways of attacking the cost-containment problem that offer very real possibilities of success over the long run.

One positive approach to the rising cost of health care—but one that obviously cannot produce results immediately—is simply this: Do everything possible to make sure that people have less need for medical and hospital care because they are in *better health*—by, for example, encouraging them to take part in programs to reduce hypertension or stop the smoking habit.

An encouraging development has been the growing number of company-sponsored "wellness" programs (see later in this chapter). It should go without saying that, in addition to all the self-evident values of seeing that people are in good health, a healthier group of employees will cost a company less for health insurance—whatever plan it may use.

A second answer to the cost problem long term may be the health maintenance organization (HMO) concept. For one thing, by their special emphasis on health *maintenance*, the HMOs aim at preventing health problems before they become more expensive. Today, after a long period of relative inattention, we are finally seeing more emphasis on health maintenance organizations as alternatives to traditional forms of medical care.

HEALTH MAINTENANCE ORGANIZATIONS

For many years, HMOs, despite the many logical arguments in their favor, had to face one troublesome problem: They usually were more expensive than conventional medical plans, so that employees themselves had to pay the difference between the cost of their company's insured plan and that of an HMO. Now the tide seems to be turning. In the last few years, the differences between HMO rates and premiums for insurance company and Blue Cross/Blue Shield fee-for-service plans have been narrowing. And, in some parts of the country, HMOs may now be cheaper. At first glance, this might seem to be a major breakthrough in cost containment. However, many other factors must be considered. For example, in its early years an HMO may skim the "cream" off the employee population—the younger, healthier people. But as time goes by, and the HMO's membership includes more of the older workers, its costs may go up.

The basic HMO idea—providing a complete range of medical care for a fixed monthly fee—is little more than half a century old. The first real start was California's Kaiser plan, which is today by far the country's largest HMO (with more than five million members). But national attention only arrived with the Health Maintenance Organization Act of 1973, which decreed that any employer of more than 25 people must offer a "dual choice" to its employees. This means that if a company is contributing to an employee health-insurance plan and there is an approved HMO operating it its area, the company must give its employees the choice of using this HMO instead of the regular company medical plan. And, for each employee who joins an HMO, the company must pay the same amount toward the HMO's charges as it would have paid to the regular medical plan.

Although the law was well intended, the results were slow in arriving. In the beginning, the rules as to how a new HMO became officially "qualified" were very strict, and a number of the early ones ran into well-publicized financial distress. But now the shakeout period seems about over, leaving the industry on a more solid footing. Even Blue Cross itself has become a major sponsor of new HMOs. And, in recent years, the number of HMO members has been increasing at a relatively fast pace, especially in the Far West.

An HMO can operate either as an *independent practice association*—a group of physicians of different specialties who work together but retain their own independent offices—or, more commonly, it will have its own self-standing facility. Here, HMO members can receive medical services from a panel of staff physicians—often including preventive care and physical checkups not usually covered by conventional health insurance. For more serious problems, the HMO is affiliated with one or more nearby hospitals, where members are treated—usually without additional charge.

This arrangement is designed to encourage HMO members to seek medical attention earlier, since the questions of finding the right kind of specialist and paying first-dollar charges are eliminated. Also, there obviously is no financial incentive for an HMO physician to recommend elective surgery or borderline hospital care. And for many HMO members there's another big plus: no reimbursement forms to fill out!

Using an HMO does have certain disadvantages, however. In the first place, the whole idea is feasible only if there is one within a convenient distance—and many areas are still outside the reach of the present network of HMOs. Even more important to many people may be the lack of choice.

You're limited to using the physicians on the HMO's own staff—which can be a problem if you have already established a good relationship with another doctor. Finally, an HMO—particularly one in financial difficulty—that puts *too much* emphasis on cost control may find itself scrimping and saving its way into overcrowded, assembly-line facilities or even medical care of unacceptably low quality.

On balance, however, the advantages of the HMO concept appear to outweigh significantly the potential drawbacks. And current trends seem to indicate that many people agree. Many companies are thus beginning to realize that they should do more than just give the required lip service to the local HMO. Instead, they are helping their employees make an intelligent decision about whether an HMO may be the best alternative for their families.

SOME THINGS TO CONSIDER ABOUT HEALTH INSURANCE
Why make it any more complicated than necessary?
Anyone who has had the difficult chore of writing a readable employee benefits booklet—especially one that is (as the law insists) understandable by the "average participant"—knows how difficult it is to explain a company's health-insurance program. In too many cases there is a multiplicity of plans and coverages, and, no matter how hard you try to explain exactly what plan covers what illness, employees often end up having to puzzle things out for themselves. Simplicity would seem to be a virtue here—and any company that has complicated multiple coverage could do its employees a favor by reappraising its entire health-insurance package.

And must the forms be so complicated?
It sometimes seems that health-insurance forms are as complicated as the plans themselves. Can it be that this is deliberate, in order to discourage people from filling them out—and thus pass up small reimbursements that aren't worth the headaches involved? Unless this really is the

motivation, a company might consider taking the time to redesign its claim forms so that they are easier to use. Why, for instance, should an employee have to write in his own company's name and address each time he submits a form? In the long run, it certainly would seem cheaper to redesign forms than to hire benefits counselors to help employees fill them out.

What's really the best way to share costs?
The simplest way to trim expenses, after all, is simply to cut back drastically on what a health insurance plan provides, and narrow it down to the most basic kinds of coverage. In fact, it has even been suggested that the entire concept of health insurance, as we now know it, could be radically altered and changed into catastrophic insurance only. Why not treat health insurance like casualty insurance: Eliminate repayments for all small charges but reimburse for everything over some fixed annual amount, such as, say, $1,000?

But it's always hard to turn the clock back. Certain kinds of medical care that once were thought of as "frills" have entered the mainstream. And most employees, like it or not, have become accustomed to conventional health-insurance Without it, they might fail to get proper medical attention when they needed it most—at the first stages of a potentially serious illness.

As we have explained, less drastic cost-sharing devices are available—especially splitting the premium cost and using deductibles or coinsurance. Nothing, however, will be especially welcomed by employees; they'll inevitably view any such cost-cutting measures as "givebacks." Labor unions, especially, have traditionally favored first-dollar coverage in the health-insurance plans they have negotiated, and will fight strenuously against anything that appears to be something less. (Recent history has shown that some unions will even accept a cut in pay before a cut in health benefits.)

Another possible solution to the cost-sharing problem (and to a number of others) is the development of a flexible benefits program, as we shall explain at some length in

Chapter 3. Oddly enough, the very employees who complain most vehemently when told they must begin to pay for something that had been free will voluntarily sign up for better coverage—even when it costs more.

But what's the "fairest" solution?
Since sickness and accidents strike rich and poor alike without discrimination, any health-insurance program does raise questions of fairness. For one thing, any shifting of costs to employees will hit lower-paid people harder. One suggested solution is to set up sliding scales for coinsurance percentages and deductibles, so that higher-paid employees will pay a larger share. But this seems to raise more problems than it solves. Gross pay is not always the best indication of a family's financial status—especially in these days of two-earner families. And aren't there enough caste distinctions in a company without installing still another one?

Just how much medical care should a plan cover?
This is a tough question. As with many other benefits, it really depends on a company's overall employee benefits philosophy. If the primary objective is simply to do an adequate job of protecting employees against dire emergencies, a "barebones" medical plan—even the catastrophic plan mentioned above—will probably suffice. On the other hand, if you want the employee-relations and recruiting impact of a really outstanding program, adding a few frills may be worth the cost.

And here, again, the flexible benefits concept makes it possible to offer both of the above: (1) a basic form of health insurande to those employees who aren't interested in anything else and (2) a much more complete program for those who want it—and are willing to pay for it.

What about government intervention in health insurance?
Recent tax reform proposals have eyed health insurance as a potential source of tax revenue, and fending off these challenges may be a difficult battle.

A more dormant issue is that of national health insurance—something that has been around a long time but has not received much attention recently. It's difficult to anticipate whether there will ever be much popular pressure for a government-sponsored program, but the fact that millions of American workers—an estimated 15 percent of the population—are still not covered by private health plans always keeps this a possibility.

Another potential problem may arise from the laws that have been passed in some states (such as Massachusetts and Illinois) to require that all health insurance plans include specific coverage for psychotherapy, well-baby care, alcoholism treatment, or whatever. A movement is under way to extend this kind of mandatory coverage on a national basis.

But what will ensure the best possible health care?

It would be very nice if there were some way to guarantee that a health-insurance plan provided everyone with the best possible medical attention at the lowest possible price. Unfortunately, that must remain an impossible dream.

How can a layman judge whether one doctor or one hospital is better than another? How much control does a patient really have over what his doctor recommends? Medicine, unfortunately, is one field where most laymen are at a disadvantage...and where high price is no guarantee of high quality.

To Sum Up

- Health-insurance, to many employees, can be the most valuable benefit they receive from their company. It is the one that is most current; the one that is most likely to be used by both employees and their families. And it is one of the few benefits that employees may actually consider when deciding whether to join one company rather than another.
- Costs are a major—and fast-growing—problem with this benefit. They won't go away, and they'll probably get worse.

But beware of easy answers. Shifting the cost burden from employer to employees isn't a long-run solution to a national problem. (However, that doesn't mean that employees should necessarily get a free ride and pay nothing at all.)
- Each employee's family needs for medical and hospital care will vary greatly—with no particular correlation to rank or pay. That's why health insurance seems to be a prime candidate for inclusion in any benefits program that offers employees some elements of choice.
- The health maintenance organization concept seems, after a number of years of trying to gain a foothold, to have finally become a serious factor in American medical care. Any company would be ill-advised to ignore the HMO's possibilities.
- And, for the long run, the best thing a company can do to decrease its health-insurance expenditures may be to see that its employees are healthier in the first place.

OTHER KINDS OF HEALTH PROTECTION

Almost every American employer of any size provides some sort of health-insurance plan. And many are now doing even more for their employees' health protection. These additional programs, in general, fall into two categories: auxiliary health services—dental, vision care, and prescription-drug plans; and preventive health programs—physical examinations, "wellness" programs, and employee assistance programs.

We have lumped both kinds of programs together here for convenience, but they actually have quite different reasons for their current popularity. The first group—the auxiliary health services—include some of those special, attention-getting benefits that often will make one company's program stand out in its area or among its competitors. They aren't really necessary, but these programs are not too expensive, either—especially when compared to such benefits as a pension plan or a conventional health-insurance program. However, as has often been pointed out, anything that is of genuine value to an employee will be perceived as a desirable employee benefit—whether it costs the company millions of dollars or virtually nothing.

The programs in the second group are designed to have long-range value to both a company and its employees. Again, their cost is relatively small, but, when one considers the potential savings in preventing more serious and more expensive health problems, they would appear to be very worthwhile.

DENTAL INSURANCE

Dental-care plans are a relatively new development, dating back not much more than 25 years, but their recent growth has been impressive. According to one estimate, only two million people were covered by dental insurance in 1965, but this figure has now grown to about 100 million. Much of the initial pressure came from labor unions, but the majority of large companies now provide dental insurance to their employees.

Dental insurance, when a company offers it, is a very popular benefit—doubtless because, even though no one enjoys visiting the dentist, about 95 percent of the American population are afflicted with tooth decay sooner or later. Even more significantly, although only about 12 to 14 percent of the people covered by health insurance actually receive benefits in any one year, as much as 60 percent of those with dental insurance use their plan annually.

HOW IT WORKS
It's been said that, in one important aspect, a dental-insurance plan is a model for what a health-insurance plan

should be—but isn't. A dental plan puts heavy emphasis on diagnosis and prevention rather than treating a patient *after* his or her illness has become serious. And very few dental plans are 100 percent company-paid, which means that almost everyone is responsible for a copayment or deductible somewhere along the line. Moreover, the amount of reimbursement is often on a sliding scale, so that the earlier you see the dentist, the less you'll have to pay in the long run.

Dental coverage is handled primarily by insurance companies, although there are also some plans sponsored by Blue Cross/Blue Shield groups or independent dental service organizations. A number of health maintenance organizations also have set up dental clinics, and some larger companies have established their own self-funded dental-insurance programs.

Although premiums for the earlier dental plans were often entirely company-paid, it's more common today for company and employee to share the cost—particularly for family coverage. Since there's usually someone with bad teeth in any family, there isn't too much danger of "adverse selection" with a dental plan (when only those who need the benefit must sign up for it, thus distorting the cost estimates).

The provisions of a dental-insurance plan are often complicated and may include sliding scales of copayment percentages. There is almost always a deductible of some sort, although this may be as little as $25 a year per person.

An important objective here is prevention. For instance, people who see their dentists every year may pay nothing at all for routine examinations and simple fillings. But, for more elaborate dental work (which might have been avoided by early attention to their teeth), they may pay both a deductible and 50 percent of the total charge. So it is cheaper to see the dentist regularly—which is exactly the intention of the plan.

Some plans have built-in maximums that limit the amount of dental-care benefits anyone may receive in one year—or even in an entire lifetime. There may also be controls to make sure that a dentist doesn't charge more than what is "usual, customary, and reasonable" for his work. If orthodontia is included in the plan (and sometimes it isn't), there usually are stricter yearly and lifetime limits than those for other kinds of dental work. And cosmetic dentistry usually isn't covered at all.

One unusual feature of many dental plans is "predetermination"—in which a dentist is required to fill out a fairly elaborate description of any serious work he plans to do on a patient (such as anything costing more than a specified amount, such as $300). This proposed treatment—and its cost—must be approved by both patient and the plan before the dentist can go ahead with it. This sounds good in theory, but there are many emergency situations, unfortunately, when it isn't very practical to delay doing anything until after the forms have been filled out and signed.

SOME THINGS TO CONSIDER ABOUT DENTAL INSURANCE

Don't dawdle in installing a plan

Anyone who is considering adopting a new dental-insurance plan should be ready to make some quick decisions. Nothing is gained by backing and filling for months—while rumors of the impending plan spread—and then announcing that the plan will go into effect six months in the future. With that kind of scenario, almost everyone will delay having dental work done. Then, once the new plan is in operation, it will be inundated by a flood of claims.

Maximums may not serve much purpose

Often there are maximums in dental-insurance programs that are similar to the limits included in medical plans. And, like many medical maximums, they often are virtually meaningless, since so few people ever have claims that add up to the top figure (although this does happen more often with dental insurance than with medical insurance). The small amount saved by having a maximum in a dental plan should be balanced against the rather large amount of ill feeling that could be created when that one extremely unfortunate employee finds his or her benefits cut off by that maximum.

There isn't much that's really "optional"

Even though almost all dental work is elective to a certain extent, about the only real option involves timing. Cavities don't fill themselves; it's only a matter of time before discomfort overrides the natural human tendency to avoid seeing the dentist. So any aspect of a dental plan that encourages preventive care and regular visits should pay off in the long run. It is questionable, therefore, whether it makes sense to have deductibles against regular dental examinations and routine care.

VISION CARE

Vision-care plans are unique in that they cover both a service and a product—a product, in fact, that is chosen largely for aesthetic reasons. These programs are similar to dental plans, but are much less common—even though at least half of almost any employee group will eventually need eyeglasses.

Plans can be free-standing, incorporated into major medical programs, or sponsored primarily by optometrists. Most plans have specific limitations (typically, a maximum of one eye examination, one set of frames, and one set of lenses per year). Sunglasses or contact lenses (unless medically required) are usually not covered, and the plans often have a fairly strict limitation on replacement glasses.

In contrast to dental plans, vision-care plans have a definite risk of adverse selection: Someone who doesn't wear glasses and doesn't think he'll ever need them isn't likely to sign up for this kind of benefit if it means money out of his own pocket. Thus, when vision-care plans are installed the premiums are usually entirely paid by the company, so that all employees are automatically covered and the possibility of adverse selection is eliminated.

Another fairly common practice is to lump vision care into a catch-all plan that includes other benefits, such as dental insurance or examinations for hearing aids—under the assumption, perhaps, that the employees with bad eyes won't be the same ones who have bad teeth or defective hearing.

Cost figures in this area are rather elusive. No "usual, customary, and reasonable" price exists for a pair of glasses. A common solution, therefore, is for the plan to pay only a scheduled dollar amount; anyone who wants designer frames must pay the difference.

PRESCRIPTION-DRUG PLANS

Aside from union pressure, there may be several reasons to install a separate prescription-drug plan—even though reimbursement for these drugs is often already included in a company's major medical plans. In the first place, many employees may not realize that prescriptions are covered by their regular plan. Or, if they do, the complications of filling out forms may discourage them from applying for relatively small repayments, even when they are entitled to them. So a special prescription-drug plan can be another inexpensive extra benefit that employees may appreciate much more than ones that cost many times as much.

To the employee, what is really attractive about a prescription-drug plan is that it provides rather complete coverage for a frequently used medical service. In fact, it may actually be an inducement to have a necessary prescription filled in the first place. (An estimated 25 percent of all doctors' prescriptions are never filled; another 10 percent are filled but never picked up.)

Most prescription plans use a fixed deductible for each prescription—which is another way of saying that the total cost of any prescription is always the same small, fixed amount: $1, $2, $2.50, or whatever. However, rising drug prices make these fixed-deductible arrangements increasingly expensive. One commonly used cost-containment approach is to encourage employees to buy generic drugs rather than brand-name products, whenever possible.

Some plans have made special agreements with groups of participating pharmacies or have established their own charge-card systems for the purchase of drugs. It's also a common practice to offer regular supplies of "maintenance" drugs for diabetes, high blood pressure, etc., via mail order. Many health maintenance organizations have arrangements for members to obtain prescription drugs at little or no cost; some even have their own pharmacies.

A few prescription-drug plans take a different approach to pricing and base their reimbursement rates on "usual, customary, and reasonable" charges. The volatility of drug prices, and the wide range from pharmacy to pharmacy, unfortunately makes this a difficult course to pursue.

With all plans, there are limitations. To prevent overuse a plan will almost always place a limit on the amount of any one drug that may be purchased, and most plans do not cover over-the-counter drugs, appliances, and the like.

PHYSICAL EXAMINATIONS

Even within the medical profession, there is controversy over whether regular physical examinations are an effective way to detect and treat unsuspected ailments. Some physicians insist that if you don't have any definite symptoms a physical exam probably won't turn up anything. Others feel that it's a good idea for everyone to be examined by a doctor at regular intervals—although doing this every year may not really be necessary, especially for younger people.

In any case, it's generally agreed that, once people reach a certain age, regular examinations are probably advisable. Many companies have a standard policy of offering physical exams to all executives above a certain level, but it isn't yet common practice to offer them routinely to all employees. (Although, as we mentioned, physical exams usually are included in the free services provided to all members of health maintenance organizations.)

Who should get them?

With today's increased emphasis on preventive medicine, a company may decide that company-paid physical examinations are a relatively inexpensive employee benefit that can result in a general long-term improvement in the health of its employees—with, over the years, less need for more expensive medical and hospital care. Once this decision is made, there arises the question of exactly which employees should receive the exams. The traditional guideline—offering them on the basis of rank alone—may be a rather limiting policy. If the benefit is worthwhile for executives, it would seem equally worthwhile for everyone—thus putting physical exams in the category of sound preventive medicine, rather than just another executive perk.

Who should perform them?

Except for the HMOs, almost all conventional health-insurance plans specifically exclude physical checkups as a benefit. This presents three alternatives: in-house medical departments, outside check-up centers or clinics, and reimbursement of employees' own physicians.

Establishing an in-house medical department staffed by doctors and/or nurses who are regular company employees is not a new idea. In the past, such a department was often limited to giving routine preemployment physicals and taking care of minor illnesses and accidents. Today, however, many companies have set up full-fledged medical departments that are responsible for both periodic employee physical examinations and other activities such as health-education programs, immunization, and counseling. (Obviously, this undertaking is possible only in a fairly large company.)

Examinations performed by staff physicians are easier to arrange and cost considerably less than those done elsewhere. An in-house medical staff can also efficiently follow up a physical, if necessary, and provide greater continuity of care. One problem, however, may be that employees will feel less comfortable in dealing with medical people who are seen as part of their employer's staff. (The old image of the "company doctor," unfortunately, was often that of someone whose principal duty was to ferret out malingerers.)

An alternative to an in-house medical department is to have employees' physicals handled by a local hospital clinic or independent physical examination service, if one is available. Although this is less expensive overall, the cost of each exam will obviously be greater. There's less opportunity for follow-ups, but employees may feel that an outside service provides more confidentiality.

Finally, the simplest procedure may be simply to offer to reimburse employees for the cost of examinations by their own physicians. This sounds easy enough, but it should be carefully monitored, since abuses are possible.

"WELLNESS" PROGRAMS

These could easily be the fastest-growing aspect of the long-term campaign to improve the general health of American workers. And wellness programs, as we have emphasized, represent one of the few ways of really combatting the rising cost of medical care. They can range from inexpensive employee communications efforts to the establishment of an elaborate on-site exercise facility. (One of the best known is that of Johnson & Johnson in New Brunswick, N.J.)

Programs can involve the distribution of information about good health practices and the sponsoring of in-house courses in such areas as weight control, nutrition, stress management, first aid, cardiopulmonary resuscitation, or how to quit smoking. Or a company may publicize health-education programs that are offered outside and reimburse employees for the costs of attending them. Also valuable can be company-sponsored screening programs for high blood pressure, early cancer detection, glaucoma, diabetes, and the like.

A wellness program seems to be among the least controversial of all employee benefits. The long-range rewards will certainly far exceed the modest sums that must be invested; what a company does to promote good employee health should be limited only by its financial resources. Almost always it must be the company's own money that pays the bills, since very few group insurance plans cover preventive programs of this kind.

However, there's one potential possible danger: creating the impression that a company cares more about the health of its executives than about that of the rest of the staff. (One major New York bank, for instance, has long had a very well-equipped and professionally staffed exercise facility that is a model of its kind...but open only to its thousand-odd vice presidents.)

EMPLOYEE-ASSISTANCE PROGRAMS

A few large companies have long had internal counseling staffs to help employees with special personal problems. But only recently have employee-assistance programs become a fairly widespread health benefit—enough to have acquired their own acronym (EAP). General Motors, in fact, is said to have as many as 100 staff psychologists to counsel its employees.

Companies have come to realize that some problems—alcoholism, drug abuse, and mental illness, in particular—can be extremely costly to a company in absenteeism, poor performance, on-the-job accidents...to say nothing of increased health and disability-insurance premiums. It's important to have assistance at hand for employees who are endangered by any of these. A good counseling program can also alleviate less obvious (but potentially just as costly) problems such as depression due to marital, family, or financial problems.

All these problems, unfortunately, are more widespread than one might wish. Companies with employee-assistance programs have discovered that as much as 10 to 20 percent of their staff will make use of them during the year.

A constant problem with any employee-assistance program

is: How do you get the people who need it to use it? Many employees will voluntarily seek assistance but, all too often, the person suffering from a serious problem such as alcoholism may be the last to recognize or admit it. Therefore, a good employee-assistance program must include the education of supervisors, so that they can recognize when one of their people has a problem—and how the company is prepared to help.

A complete employee-assistance program for a large company may include the professional services of physicians, psychologists, psychiatrists, social workers, and other specialists. Most employers, of course, can't establish an elaborate in-house program, but they can make sure that someone is available to meet emergency situations. When necessary, employees can be referred to the proper outside agencies that offer a wide variety of expert help and, perhaps most important, guarantee greater confidentiality.

One note of caution, however: Don't oversell what an employee-assistance program can accomplish. No matter how well intended, it can't do everything. Some problems, unfortunately, may be much too serious for an EAP to handle—and employees shouldn't expect it to.

To Sum Up

- Auxiliary health-care services such as dental, vision, and prescription-drug programs are all relatively modest in cost (at least compared to regular medical insurance); however, they are very visible employee benefits that are used often to take care of relatively small expenses. For those employees who do take advantage of them, they will be perceived as extremely valuable. So, if the objective of an overall benefits program is to help create a very positive image with employees, these can be well worth the expense.
- Of the three, a dental plan is the most likely to be used; it also has the distinct advantage of having built-in financial incentives that encourage good dental health practices.

- The new wellness and employee-assistance programs have indisputable long-term value, and a company would seem quite short-sighted to ignore them entirely. The only question should be just how far to go in this direction.
- Physical examinations are something of a borderline case; although their value for younger employees is not certain, it seems advisable for older ones to get regular checkups, either in-house or outside. And this applies regardless of rank.

LIFE INSURANCE

Life insurance really isn't much fun. Perhaps because it's a classic no-win situation: either you keep paying money over the years but never see any benefit from it, or your life insurance *does* pay off—which (at least as far as you're concerned) is much, much worse. Nevertheless, life insurance seems here to stay. It can be very comforting to know that there will be some kind of financial protection for your survivors if you should die unexpectedly.

Group life insurance was one of the very first benefits that employers offered to their workers; the earliest formal group insurance plan was set up by the Pantasote Leather Company through the Equitable Life Assurance Society in 1911.

HOW IT WORKS

In the beginning, the chief reason for providing life insurance was probably an effort to do a bit more than simply pass the hat when someone died on the job. But the amount of insurance was usually no more than a few thousand dollars to help pay funeral expenses and provide some financial help to the bereaved family for a few months. As group life insurance became commonplace, this same reasoning continued. In most cases, the early life-insurance policies paid out a fixed sum of dollars to the family of anyone who died.

More recently, however, group life insurance has taken on a different pattern. Most companies now provide an insurance benefit that is based directly on each employee's salary. The amount of coverage is governed by base salary; it's equal to one, two, or (sometimes) three or more times a year's pay. Only in a relatively few companies do people still get a fixed amount across the board, and in these cases it's often because of a long-standing union contract. (For some reason, many unions have not been very aggressive in negotiating more generous life-insurance benefits.) This system is simple and easy to control, but as we shall see later, it may result in too little insurance for some employees and too much for others—which makes everyone slightly unhappy.

A curious vestige of the "pass the hat to pay funeral expenses" idea still remains in the Social Security program. If you have any kind of Social Security coverage (and that, of course, includes the great majority of working people in the United States) your family is entitled to a flat sum of $255—no more, no less—when you die. The only people who don't get this benefit are those who die without a living spouse or dependents.

Objectives

Even today's generous amounts of group life insurance can't do very much for a deceased employee's family over the long term. The announced goal of a company's life-insurance plan may be something like "to allow survivors to maintain their standard of living." But this isn't very realistic. A lump sum of a year's salary—or even two or three years'—certainly helps, but it can't, all by itself, "maintain" much of a standard of living for very long. The real financial support for an employee's surviving dependents must come from other kinds of benefits—ones that provide more permanent protection than will a lump sum from life insurance.

With all its limitations, however, don't underestimate group life insurance. It's very big business for the insurance companies—amounting to almost half of all the life insurance now in effect. And the grand total of group coverage now in force for American workers is almost *two trillion dollars.*

Costs

Group life insurance is an almost perfect example of the basic mathematics of the insurance business: The larger the group of people, the more surely will operate the inexorable laws of probability. The result is that insurance company actuaries can accurately forecast just how many people can be expected to die in a given year. (The larger the group, the more likely actuarial predictions will be right.) Rates are established accordingly.

In return (assuming we're talking about a relatively typical group of employees—no coal miners, no asbestos workers), anyone, no matter how old, who joins a company's group can sign up for life insurance, without taking any kind of physical exam or answering a health questionnaire. For some people, of course, this in itself is a very attractive benefit.

Usually this privilege is restricted in one slight but important way. If their employer is *not* paying the full cost of the group's life insurance, employees have the option of choosing whether they want it. But they usually must make this decision when they begin work with a company. And, if they pass it up (or don't sign up for the full amount of insurance) at the beginning, they may have to take a physical if they change their minds later on. This, of course, is so that people who have just heard some very bad news from their doctor won't rush out to sign up for the maximum amount of life insurance.

Extent of coverage

In many companies, group life insurance is now only one of an assortment of benefits designed to help out the family of an employee who dies. There may also be an "accidental death or dismemberment" clause; there may be a business travel accident insurance plan; there may be some kind of special survivors' benefits plan; there may well be benefits under the company's pension or profit-sharing plan; and, almost certainly, there will be Social Security.

Many of these plans could overlap, especially if a large company's insurance and human resources departments have set up various kinds of insurance over time without coordinating their efforts. Or it can result from some aggressive insurance-company salesmanship. The end result may be that a company finds itself, for example, with a medical plan and a life insurance plan (two entirely different kinds of benefits) that are awkwardly linked together under a single policy. Or, going to the other extreme, a company might end up with a basic insurance plan with one insurance carrier and a "supplemental" plan with an entirely different carrier.

Types of life insurance
In the great majority of cases, the group life insurance provided to employees is *term insurance*, the simplest and cheapest variety. It will pay out a fixed amount to the beneficiary an employee has named in the event of his or her death—nothing else. However, some companies have begun to offer variations on this theme, such as *paid-up* or *universal* life insurance, which build up cash values in addition to the fixed amount of death protection.

Who pays for it?
A company may foot the entire bill for its employees' life insurance. Or it may offer to pay part of the premium and allow those people who want insurance to pay the remainder. Often there will be a combination of these methods: The employer will pay for "basic" protection—say, insurance equal to one year's salary—and an employee who wants additional coverage has the option of buying it. This extra or supplemental insurance can be equal to another year's, two years', or more salary, with the employee paying the full premium or the employer partially subsidizing the cost.

How much will it cost the employee?
Employees have two ways of paying all or a share of the cost of extra life insurance to supplement the basic amount they get for free. The easiest plan is to have a single fixed rate (some-

thing like 60 cents a month per thousand dollars of insurance, for example). This is easy to calculate and easy to explain, but not very fair or logical. The rate will be a good deal for older employees—much cheaper than any insurance they could get on their own. But it will be no bargain for younger employees, who may find that other term insurance, such as Savings Bank Life Insurance, is cheaper for them.

The alternative is to set up a schedule of age groups and charge employees progressively more for life insurance as they get older. This presents a different problem. Although the insurance will now be reasonably inexpensive for younger people, the older employees will find themselves paying rather substantial premiums—which could mean that some of the people whose families most need insurance protection are priced out of the market.

Converting group insurance to individual coverage
One of the features of almost every group insurance plan—always touted in employee benefits booklets—is the fact that employees leaving a company may convert their soon-to-expire group insurance to a regular individual life insurance policy without a medical examination. This privilege usually is only available for a limited time, such as 31 days after termination of employment.

There are a couple of problems, however. The employee who is interested will soon discover that the "regular" policy is much more expensive than was the company group insurance (particularly if the company plan was free!). And, unless someone anticipates being unemployed for quite a while, why bother? Your next employer will almost surely have a group life insurance plan of *some* kind. As a result, only about one percent of employees bother to convert their group life insurance.

Tax regulations
In the old preinflation days—when a yearly salary of $50,000 was rather impressive and company-paid group insurance equal to no more than a year's salary was more-or-less

standard—only a fortunate few were aware of one curious feature of the federal tax laws. But by now many more people have discovered that the premiums their company pays for life-insurance coverage above the $50,000 level are, under the law, deemed to be taxable income (an unpleasant surprise to someone making $30,000 a year with company-paid life insurance equal to two years' salary).

Of course, the amount in question usually isn't very large. The IRS rates are based on age, so that someone 42 years old with $100,000 of company-paid life-insurance coverage, for example, is receiving "imputed income" of only about $200 a year. Not much—but taxable income nevertheless. In the higher brackets, of course, this regulation can create a rude shock at W-2 time. And, perhaps more unsettling, it may be an unwelcome forerunner of the tax treatment of other employee benefits in the future.

Accidental death and dismemberment (AD&D) insurance

One rather grisly aspect of group life insurance is the typical policy's "accidental death or dismemberment" clause. It has long been traditional for insurance companies to pay a family more if its loved one dies in an accident rather than from natural causes. (Remember the old James M. Cain book and movie *Double Indemnity?*) Things haven't changed; modern group policies still offer to pay double (or even more) for accidental death. This actually doesn't increase the premium very much; there really aren't as many accidental deaths as one might imagine—despite the publicity when a particularly nasty one occurs. The National Safety Council recently estimated that the death rate from accidents in the United States is at its lowest level in 70 years.

Payments aren't limited to death benefits, either. Some policies offer to pay lifetime benefits to people who are totally disabled in an accident. However, since (as we shall explain in the next section) there are many other potential sources of income for these unfortunate people, the benefits to be received under group life insurance may be somewhat illusory.

The "dismemberment" provision must be a relic of the time when ghastly industrial accidents were all too common. Most employee benefits booklets still have a fascinating section elucidating how much you would get for such unfortunate combinations as the loss of one leg and one arm, an eye and a foot, and the like. (Usually, it's some fixed percentage of what your life is worth, if that's any comfort.)

Looking at them logically, none of the accidental death benefits seem to make too much sense. However, it's almost routine to find an "AD&D" clause tacked onto a group life insurance policy, which will immediately increase the benefits if the covered person dies in an accident. Whether this is worth the extra cost is quite questionable. And the cost of AD&D, small as it is, may still be far out of proportion to the chances of it ever paying off.

Travel accident insurance
This is another very popular extra that companies seem to include routinely in their insurance programs without much serious thought—even when they already have an AD&D clause in their group life insurance. Accidental death is rare enough—death while traveling is even less frequent. And some companies go even further: it must be *business travel*; if you were just on vacation, you're out of luck. The sums paid out for one of these rare kinds of death are truly impressive: often as much as four times salary—on top of all the regular life insurance.

Insurance for dependents
Many group insurance policies offer employees the option of covering their spouse or children with separate life insurance on their own lives. However, the amounts provided are nowhere near as much as that of the main policy—usually only a few thousand dollars. This seems to be another vestige of the "funeral expenses" proposition: just enough to give a child a decent burial. It would seem to have outlived its usefulness, but insurance companies offer this coverage at very modest premiums (owing to the equally modest chance of

payment)—and some people still seem to want it, perhaps out of habit.

SOME THINGS TO CONSIDER ABOUT LIFE INSURANCE
What do people really need?
That's the key question—one that underlies the whole concept of group life insurance. Some people require a fairly substantial amount of life insurance to protect their families, such as the young married man with a nonworking wife, a couple of small children, and a heavily mortgaged house (the classic "typical" employee, if you will). And, of course, there are many less-traditional families today who need insurance just as much: single parents of both sexes, people with aged dependent parents, and the like.

By contrast, there are always a substantial number of employees in a company who have little or no need for life insurance: single employees without dependents, people with spouses in well-paying jobs, those who are adequately covered by other insurance or financial resources. For these people, the money that their company contributes for life-insurance protection might better be spent on some other kinds of benefits.

Should all employees have the same coverage?
The customary, all-too-easy life-insurance practice is to have one blanket program that covers everyone with the same level of company-paid life insurance, regardless of their individual needs or desires. Today, this seems rather wasteful. For some people, it is still too little; for others, it's much more than they need. A more sensible solution, it seems, would be to give employees a modest amount of free insurance and let them pay all or part of the cost of any additional life insurance they want. It might be better still to offer employees the option of choosing extra life insurance as an alternative to some other benefit—as part of a flexible employee benefits program (see Chapter 4).

Under either of these plans, the people who really want and need life insurance will be the ones who sign up for it—and, by paying part of the cost, should appreciate it more. And, for an employer, there's much more employee-relations mileage to be gained for each dollar spent on premiums.

Should insurance coverage be based on salary?
We have come to accept the fact that group life insurance can be one of the few employee benefits that is directly tied to salary level. Even government tax regulations specifically permit this practice and declare it to be nondiscriminatory.

However, several alternatives to basing life insurance strictly on pay level are possible. The minimum amount of free life insurance given to all employees could be a fixed dollar amount rather than be related to salary. Or one or more different variables might be considered in determining each person's coverage: age, salary, and whether an employee had dependents. Under such an arrangement, for example, a 40-year-old employee with dependents might get free insurance equal to two years' salary, while one 60 years old with no dependents might get insurance equal to only half a year's salary.

Why should it make any difference how you die?
Under many group insurance plans, as we have seen, the circumstances of someone's death can play an all-too-important role in determining how much the survivors will receive. If the death is in an accident, the beneficiaries may often get two or three times as much as they would if death were from a natural cause. And dying while traveling on company business may be a veritable bonanza. Here's a horrible example of how this all might work.

Let's imagine a company with a fairly typical company-paid group insurance policy—providing an amount equal to two years' salary when an employee dies, with an extra payment of an additional two years' salary for accidental death, plus another double amount (an extra four years' salary altogether) for death on business travel. (These are, in fact, relatively modest provisions; some accident and business travel policies pay even more.) Let's pick two employees, Mrs. A and Mrs. B.

Mrs. A has been with the company just six months, and is a computer expert earning $50,000 a year. She's 40 years old and married to Dr. A, a surgeon with an annual income of $150,000. The A's have no children.

Mrs. B is a secretary who has worked for the company for 15 years and now makes a salary of $25,000. She's also 40 years old, but is divorced and has two small children, now 8 and 10 years old, whom she must support alone.

Neither of these women, obviously, represents the "typical" American working family for whom most insurance policies were originally designed—but they certainly aren't impossible to imagine in today's business world. Now let's have tragedy strike both families: While driving to the airport for a company business trip, Mrs. A has an accident and is instantly killed. Mrs. B is the victim of cancer and dies after a long, painful illness.

What does this company's group insurance plan do for their survivors? Because Mrs. A died in an accident and on business travel, the policy pays off at the six-times-annual-salary rate. So Dr. A gets a check for $300,000. But Mrs. B's children are not so fortunate; they receive only $50,000—two times her salary, with no extras for accidental death or business travel.

Well, you say, life is unfair. And we *have* loaded the dice in presenting these two soap-opera scenarios. But, unfortunately, this is exactly what would happen today under many a supposedly generous and well-thought-out company group insurance plan.

What about life insurance after retirement?
Obviously, if everyone—no matter how old—were covered by life insurance, everyone's survivor would eventually collect. And that's part of the problem with continuing life insurance for employees after they retire. The simple solution, of course, would be to say goodbye to retiring employees and

end their life-insurance summarily. It could be rationalized that most retirees, with grown children and paid-off mortgages, have fewer financial responsibilities—especially if they are about to receive a generous company pension plus Social Security. But this isn't always the case, of course. Many retirees actually have *increasing* financial problems, and, to many potential widows or widowers, a life-insurance payment is a simple matter of financial survival. Even worse, the cost of individual life insurance for anyone in this age bracket—assuming it were available—could be almost prohibitive.

Fortunately, there are some alternatives to cutting off retiring employees' insurance when they leave. Life insurance can be continued after people retire, but with the amount of coverage diminishing according to some fixed scale (10 percent a year, for example). Oe a company might, over the years they work, invest regularly in paid-up life insurance for each employee instead of the customary term insurance. This costs more, but retirees would end up with insurance coverage after they retire at no continuing expense to their company.

To Sum Up

- Life insurance can be an extremely important benefit—but only to a limited group of people. So it might be wise for a company to let those who most need life insurance pay for it themselves at low group rates. Or, better, make this a company-paid benefit that employees may choose as an alternative to some other benefit.
- It might be time to reexamine the traditional practice of having life-insurance coverage indexed to each employee's salary level, with an automatic increase in benefits each time salary goes up. Is this really a good way to reward improved performance?
- The actual value of such timeworn insurance products as

"accidental death and dismemberment" clauses, business travel insurance, and modest life-insurance coverage for employees' dependents should be carefully investigated. They're cheap enough, but probably of very limited value.
- Providing life insurance for retired employees can be a dangerous financial trap that will get no better with time, as the retired population increases and government attention becomes more likely. Long-term planning is vital here.

LONG-TERM DISABILITY INSURANCE

Long-term disability insurance—or LTD, as it is commonly known—might be called the stepchild of the benefits family. Because so few people, fortunately, ever take advantage of it, LTD is almost ignored in many discussions of employee benefits. Yet, in some important ways, LTD is actually one of the most important benefits of all—for it does exactly what insurance is supposed to do: taking advantage of mathematical probability, it protects a group of people, at very low cost, against a potentially devastating disaster to one of them.

This sort of insurance actually has a long history, dating all the way back to the European guilds and fraternal societies. These groups were often set up for the express purpose of taking care of those members unfortunate enough to suffer a crippling disability—which, of course, happened all too frequently in those days. In this country, the first formal long-term disability provision was that included by Montgomery Ward in its group life-insurance policy back in 1911. Today, most company benefit programs offer some sort of LTD insurance, although it may be less than adequate, either in the amounts it pays or the number of people it covers.

Perhaps the very thought of spending the remainder of one's days incapacitated and unable to earn a living is so painful to contemplate that, for most people, the best solution is to take an "it can't happen to me" approach to the possibility of long-term disability. This flies in the face of statistics, however. For someone between the ages of 30 and 50, there's a much greater chance of being disabled for 90 days or more than there is of dying.

Much the same attitude can prevail in planning an employee benefits program. The chances of long-term disability ever striking seem so remote that scant attention is paid to insurance against its happening. And thus LTD insurance is, all too often, relegated to the list of optional benefits, rather than remaining in the first rank.

HOW IT WORKS

Like other forms of group insurance, LTD coverage operates on the familiar share-the-risk principle: a small premium is charged to all members of the group; a large amount will be paid out to those few who need it. Because, in this case, the risk that any one person will actually suffer long-term disability is very small, the premiums are relatively modest.

Who pays for it?
There are three possibilities: The company can pay the entire premium; the insurance can be paid in full by the employees who want this kind of coverage; or employer and employee can split the costs. In the last two cases, an employee's share of the premium is customarily deducted from his or her paycheck. Claims are infrequent, and administration is relatively simple, but the few claims that do occur may involve rather complex medical ramifications and long-term payment responsibilities and monitoring. Therefore, most companies find it easiest to put their LTD in the hands of an outside insurance company that specializes in this field.

Benefits
The benefits that a disabled employee receives from LTD insurance are almost always directly related to the salary he or she was making at the time of becoming disabled. The monthly amount thus is usually calculated as a percentage of pay—anywhere from 50 to 80 percent, with 60 percent being

most common. There is also a maximum amount, which may, in fact, be relatively low—especially if an LTD policy has never been adjusted for inflation. Lying behind these percentages, of course, is one important consideration: Under the law, disability benefits are usually tax free, so anything above 70 or 80 percent of salary might well provide a worker with greater real income than when he or she worked full time.

Because of its very nature—"long-term insurance"—this is one benefit for which timing is most important. When LTD begins, how long it lasts, and when it ends are all important variables to be considered. In most cases, there is a fairly long time lapse before a sick or injured employee is eligible for LTD—it may be a specified number of months, such as five or six, or coverage may begin only after other benefits, such as a company's short-term disability payments or salary continuation, have ended.

Although some earlier forms of LTD insurance kept paying for only a specified number of years, the more usual practice now is for coverage to continue as long as the disability does—or until the disabled employee is eligible for benefits from the company's pension plan. (Under many private pension plans, an employee continues to accumulate years of pension service credit even while disabled and unable to work.)

Coordination with other disability programs

Long-term disability insurance must face one special problem: the other assistance programs for which a disabled worker may often (although not always) qualify. These can include public programs such as Social Security's Disability Insurance, state disability programs, and workers' compensation. A disabled worker may, in some cases, be eligible for payments from a company's other benefits plans, such as travel accident insurance, the "accidental death or dismemberment" clause of a life insurance policy, or a disability provision under the pension plan.

The overall problem here, of course, is to make sure that

someone doesn't obtain benefits from several sources that, taken together, add up to more than 100 percent of what his or her previous salary had been. But all of these programs have different rules for eligibility, different time limits, and even different definitions of disability. Coordinating them is never an easy task. Social Security usually presents the most difficult coordination problems. Do you count an employee's basic Social Security benefit or the maximum family benefit? What do you do when Social Security benefits change? Or when eligibility rules are tightened? How do you handle the fact that Social Security benefits usually are weighted to favor lower-paid employees? Do you include Medicare benefits?

A definition problem
One gray area that surrounds long-term disability insurance is the matter of the very definition of "disability" itself—upon which major amounts of benefits payments can somtimes hinge. Does this mean not being able to work at your regular occupation? At a similar but less physically demanding job for which you are qualified? Or not being able to work at all?

Some insurance plans use a sliding scale of definitions: For the first two years, perhaps, you are eligible for LTD insurance if you can't do your regular job; after two years, however, your benefits end if you are physically able to do some other job for which your training and experience have prepared you. Some LTD programs may provide for rehabilitation and retraining workers for new jobs that will take them off the disability list.

This question of defining disability can be a crucial one. In recent years Social Security, simply by using a stricter definition, has disqualified many recipients from further benefits.

SOME THINGS TO CONSIDER ABOUT LTD INSURANCE
Is the vital role of LTD too often underestimated?
The fact that so many companies make LTD an optional benefit that must be paid for by employees, either partially or

entirely, is somewhat difficult to understand. Of all benefits, this is probably the one that, because of the low probability of need, is least likely to seem as important as it actually is. And thus, given the chance to save a little money by passing up LTD coverage, many employees will do just that. Is this what companies are prepared for? Do they really want their people to rely exclusively on public assistance in the event—improbable as it may be—that they become disabled for the rest of their lives?

Should LTD be reserved for higher-paid employees only?
In the past, many companies set up long-term disability programs only for top-level workers, under the theory that public programs could take care of the rank and file. (And, of course, if the programs were optional, charges of discrimination might be averted.) They also worried about the danger of "overinsuring" some of their employees. This, they feared, encouraged malingering—or, at the least, did not give people who had been out on disability much incentive to return to work.

Today, however, the dependability of public benefits is open to question, and it would seem rather hard-hearted for a company to force its employees to rely exclusively on public programs to take care of disability.

On the other hand, is LTD just a "phantom benefit"?
That's what it has been called—especially for lower-paid employees. Why? Workers in this group who are covered by their company's LTD program—and may even be paying a share of the premium—sometimes find, when they come to collect, that the entire benefit is offset by "coordination" with other programs. This can be avoided if the LTD plan provides for some sort of guaranteed minimum benefit, so that everyone will get at least *something* from the plan.

Is a flat percentage of pay the fairest benefit?
Probably not, especially if it's a percentage of gross pay before taxes. Most LTD plans pay less than 100 percent of a disabled

worker's pay because, under current law, this income is not taxable. However, as everyone knows, there are many twists and turns to the income-tax laws. And, since individual financial situations vary so widely, this is a difficult question for a company to resolve. The best answer might be for a company to provide a flat LTD benefit to everyone without charge—with additional coverage available as an option for those who need it.

To Sum Up

- Long-term disability insurance is often a much-underestimated employee benefit that actually is the classic insurance situation: At low cost, it provides protection against a catastrophe that, however unlikely, can be financially disastrous.
- Companies that have avoided providing free LTD insurance, perhaps from fears that it would merely duplicate coverage provided by other benefit plans, both public and private, might be wise to reappraise this decision.

PENSIONS

Of all the major employee benefits, pensions are probably the most controversial—the one benefit about which there are the most differences of opinion and the greatest variations in interest level. To many people (especially those senior executives who usually set up a company's benefits program) pensions are the very cornerstone of that program. On the other hand, for many other employees—particularly the younger ones—pensions are a matter of supreme indifference. They don't really expect to be working long enough at their present company ever to be eligible for a pension, whatever it may be; in fact, the very idea of retirement itself is so far in the future as to be something of almost total unconcern.

The American private pension system has a long history, dating back at least to 1759, when a retirement program was established to take care of the widows and dependents of Presbyterian ministers. The first formal industrial pension plan was that of the American Express Company in 1875, and through the early part of this century, a number of other companies followed with retirement programs for long-term employees. The motivation for all these was to recognize many years of faithful service—the gratuity or "gold watch" theory of rewarding employees who simply had become too old to work regularly and consequently had to be put out to pasture.

Even as late as the 1930s, only about 15 percent of American workers were covered by private pension plans. As a result, during the Depression many long-service employees were forced out of work with no financial support of any kind. This, of course, led to strong pressure for some sort of government-supported retirement program, which culminated in the introduction of Social Security in 1935. The movement toward private pension plans gained some headway because of the wage-control regulations of World War II, along with the new concept (approved by the Internal Revenue Service in 1942) that a company's contributions to a "qualified" retirement plan could be tax deductible.

Since then, it has been accepted almost universally that veteran employees should not simply be let go when they reach retirement age. They will have (certainly) the support of Social Security and also (with good fortune) a private pension. And, as elsewhere in the post-World War II history of employee benefits, pressure from labor unions has contributed to the growth of the private pension concept.

It isn't simply charity that is behind pension plans. Without them, veteran workers would have no choice but to work until they dropped. A pension plan can encourage orderly workforce turnover, with more opportunities for young, ambitious—and more productive—workers to move ahead as older ones retire.

Another milestone in American private pension development was the passage of the Employee Retirement Income Security Act of 1974—now familiarly known as ERISA. This legislation was enacted in response to well-publicized criticism of the private pension system and its alleged unfair treatment of workers. It set up a whole series of new standards for eligibility, vesting, funding, reporting, fiduciary responsibilities, and employee communications. ERISA covers both pension plans and other "welfare" plans and is jointly administered by the Labor and Treasury Departments.

Meanwhile, pensions themselves have become a gigantic economic force. They control capital investments of well over a trillion dollars today—including about 12 percent of all American common stocks. And the total pension investment, it is estimated, will grow to three times this size by 1995.

In fact, the total assets of some pension funds may actually be larger than they should be. Conservative financial planning and unanticipated strength in the economy in recent years have caused a number of private pension plans to be considerably overfunded—a situation that can, as we shall see later, lead to pressure for these plans to be terminated and the funds put to some "better" use.

A more controversial aspect of private pensions is the question of exactly how much protection they can provide to exactly how many people. Government surveys show that approximately 70 percent of all full-time American workers are covered by private employers' pensions. However, this figure doesn't really tell the whole story. For the individual employee, the most important consideration is whether he or she is *vested*—not simply "covered" in the technical sense.

As we shall soon explain, vesting means having a clear right to a pension benefit—something that usually doesn't occur under many pension plans until the employee has been working at the same place for 10 years. Moving to another job will mean that all the pension credit that has been "built up" under this kind of plan will vanish. However, under other types of plans, the vesting period can be considerably shorter.

HOW CONVENTIONAL PENSIONS WORK

A "pension" is simply any formal plan established by a company to provide retirement income for its workers—with, very often, other benefits earmarked for those who become disabled or for the survivors of employees who die before they retire. In taking a broad first look at pensions, we shall discuss the long-established variety that uses the *defined-benefit* principle. (Some people have called this the only genuine retirement plan.)

Pension plans, it should be noted at the beginning, provide lucrative employment for an army of experts—benefits consultants, actuaries, lawyers, accountants. And the services these people provide are all too necessary: Any layman who might naively attempt to set up a pension plan all by himself would immediately fall into a sea of troubles—particularly from the Internal Revenue Service. So we won't attempt to provide a do-it-yourself manual for constructing your own plan.

The replacement income concept

Most conventional defined-benefit pension plans start off with a basic objective—to provide "replacement income" to long-term employees. In essence, the idea is to set up a pension arrangement that will guarantee that a company's career employees will continue to receive for the rest of their lives a certain percentage of the income they were making just before they retired. This retirement income will include both a company pension *and* Social Security, but, of course, the replacement percentage will almost always be somewhat less than 100 percent, since it's assumed that people will need less income after they retire than they did before.

The concept of replacement is designed to apply only to those who retire after a long stretch of continuous service with one company; usually this means 30 years or more. It represents a "deferred wage" that they have earned over their years of service to that company.

It's important to recognize that replacement income involves a mathematical formula that applies to everyone's pension calculation. Whether or not this formula will yield an adequate retirement income depends entirely on the individual. After all, everyone's personal financial situation is different—one person may retire with a paid-off mortgage and a spouse still earning a good income; someone else, with exactly the same preretirement salary, may retire owing large monthly payments to several banks and be the sole support of two children attending expensive colleges.

No prearranged mathematical formula can determine the "replacement" percentage that will be adequate for each of them. However, if a pension is intended to provide a pre-established monthly income to career employees who retire, it must use something as a guideline. And, so far, no one seems to have come up with anything better than the replacement ratio idea.

A typical pension formula
Almost every defined-benefit pension uses a formula based on years of service and salary to arrive at a certain dollar amount for a retiree's pension. This formula can be a relatively simple one or, more often than not, one that is quite complicated.

An extremely simple formula might work like this: Suppose you decide that, for every employee with at least 30 years of service, a fair replacement ratio after retirement would be 60 percent of his or her final salary. Anyone who retires with that much service, therefore, will begin to receive a monthly pension check that is equal to 60 percent of final salary. Someone with less than 30 years' service with the company will get a prorated pension—one that is reduced, say, by two percent for each year less than 30. So someone retiring with only 25 years of service would get a pension equal to 50 percent of final salary; someone with 20 years would get 40 percent; and so forth.

But what's "final salary"?
This sounds like a pretty straightforward idea until you begin to look at it more closely; then some questions begin to arise.

First, "final salary" can actually mean a number of different things, depending on how you look at it.

Suppose, for instance, that a man happened to receive an unusually large bonus in the last year he worked—or put in for the maximum amount of overtime. Would it be fair to use this salary as the basis for a pension that will continue for the rest of his or her life? You might minimize this distortion, perhaps, by figuring pensions only on base salary—but would this be fair to employees whose regular income includes a fairly large amount of bonus pay or overtime?

Thus the usual practice has been to base pensions on an average of the last three, five, or ten years' salaries, rather than a single year. And a further provision such as "the highest five salaries in the last ten years" will avoid being unfair to people whose pay has tapered off in the last couple of years of work before retirement.

This concept—basing pension on "final average" pay—is now fairly widespread. In the past, pensions were often based on the "career average" concept, in which an employee builds up a certain amount of pension credit in each year of work, based on the actual pay received during that year—such as a pension credit equal to 1.5 percent of annual salary. This worked out fairly well before the days of raging inflation. But then a pension credit that had once seemed reasonably generous began to look pretty skimpy in terms of current dollars. (However, as inflation begins to ease, there could be a renewed interest in the career-average method.)

Other complications
Some other aspects of our seemingly simple and straightforward pension formula could lead to various inequalities affecting one group or another:

- Why stop giving credit after 30 years of service? But if you keep on giving annual additions, some long-term employees may actually end up with a pension that's larger than their final salary.
- A company may feel that a straight two-percent-for-each-

year formula won't provide enough retirement income for shorter-term employees who are hired in their forties and fifties and have no other vested pensions. One solution might be to complicate the formula with some kind of front loading—perhaps by giving a pension credit of 2 1/2 percent for each of the first 10 years of service and less after that.

- Another problem with our simple formula is that it doesn't take Social Security into consideration. If our real goal is for employees to end up with a retirement income that's a percentage of their final pay, the money they will get from Social Security must figure into the formula somehow. And this is complicated by the fact that Social Security provides a much higher percentage of final pay to people at the lower ends of the income scale. (Later, we shall discuss this question of Social Security "integration" at some length.)

All these, plus a number of other problems we haven't even mentioned, mean that, in the end, most pension formulas are rather complicated—and benefits consultants and actuaries must spend a lot of time revising them to meet changing times and changing business needs.

WHAT TO LOOK FOR IN A PENSION PLAN

Defined-benefit pension plans come in all shapes and sizes. In examining the details of a particular plan, you may observe some of the following:

Who's covered by the plan?
Which employees to cover under its pension plan is a decision each company must make, based on its own circumstances—whether to include only nonunion employees, only salaried workers, only full-time staff members, or whatever. There are, however, some rather strict rules against discriminating within these broad guidelines. The Internal Revenue Service would not

qualify—that is, give tax-deductible status to—a plan that, for example, benefited only top executives. (Although, as mentioned later in this chapter, there are nonqualified supplemental pension arrangements that can be devised for them.)

Many companies—especially those with high turnover rates for short-term employees—would probably prefer not to include people in their pension plan until they have been at work for a specified period of, say, one year. This is simply to cut down on unnecessary paperwork for a lot of short-timers who will never be eligible for pensions. (Once an employee does join the official rolls of a pension plan, all service dating back to when he or she first joined the company can be counted for plan purposes.)

Age is another question that can cause paperwork headaches, especially if there are many very young employees. As a result, many companies have also set age minimums for pension eligibility. However, the Retirement Equity Act of 1984 requires that this minimum starting point may not be higher than age 21 for the beginning of pension credits and age 18 for vesting credits.

Who is vested?

An employee's benefits are said to be "vested" under a retirement plan when they are fully guaranteed and can't be forfeited, even if that person leaves to work somewhere else. As mentioned at the beginning of this section, under a defined-benefit arrangement like those we have been discussing, employees whose pension credits are not yet vested are somewhat in limbo. Even though they are considered to be "covered" by their company's pension plan, if they leave their current employer before their pension benefits are vested, any "credit" they have built up will be canceled.

Under the provisions of the Employee Retirement Income Security Act of 1974 (ERISA), there are three different ways in which a pension plan may provide vesting. However, the great majority of defined-benefit plans now use what's known as the "cliff vesting" rule, under which no pension credit is vested until an employee has been covered by a plan for 10 years. However, once this 10-year period is up an employee is fully vested.

Thus, the employee who leaves after 10 years or more of service gets full credit for the pension that has already been earned—although it isn't necessarily payable until the plan's normal or early retirement date. But the size of this vested pension is usually frozen at the amount determined by the plan's formula; very rarely do companies pass on any future increases to former employees with vested pensions who leave to work somewhere else.

Obviously, this 10-year all-or-nothing rule will work to the disadvantage of workers who move from job to job. In this day of increasing job mobility, many people will go through their entire working careers without staying the requisite time to earn a defined-benefit pension from any one of their employers. So it's not surprising that there is growing pressure on the government to liberalize pension-vesting rules—such as to reduce the 10-year waiting period to, say, 5 years and to require some kind of "portability," so that workers can somehow carry their pension credits with them from one job to another.

Who foots the bill?
Under a defined-benefit plan, the costs are almost always borne entirely by the employer. Some time ago, many such plans required that employees also make contributions, but very few, if any, of these still exist. (Employees may, of course, contribute to a variety of other types of retirement and capital-accumulation plans, as explained in the next section.)

To make sure that money will be available in the future to cover the benefits that the plan defines, a company makes regular investments into a trust fund. Some plans—mostly ones that are relatively small in size—invest this money in individual contracts with an insurance company. Most larger firms, however, make annual trust-fund contributions that vary from year to year. The annual amount that a company contributes to cover the future obligations of its pension plan is not fixed in advance—it's a business judgment made with the advice of the company's expert advisors.

And this isn't a decision to be made lightly, for any money contributed cannot be withdrawn as long as a plan is continued. Under the law, it must be invested and used only for the plan's pension benefits. The usual arrangement is for the company's pension contributions to go to a trust fund that is operated entirely independently, with trustees designated by the sponsor but the actual investments being made by *fiduciaries* associated with some outside agency, such as a bank.

A company must make sure that it contributes enough to take care of its present and expected pension obligations—but, at the same time, not waste money by overfunding the plan. (The whole question of how to invest pension fund monies properly is an important and complicated one—but one that is outside the scope of this book.)

What is retirement age?

Most American pension plans use age 65 as the time for "normal" retirement, probably because this was arbitrarily selected for the beginning of full Social Security benefits. (It's sometimes—mistakenly—blamed on Otto von Bismarck, who instituted one of the first national retirement plans in Germany, in the 1870s.) Most companies continue to use age 65 as their pension plan's "normal retirement date," but, under the Age Discrimination in Employment Act, they must now allow most employees, if they wish, to work through age 70. (One exception: an executive entitled to an annual pension benefit of $44,000 or more, who can be forced to retire at age 65.)

This arrangement has posed a problem for some companies: What should be done with the pension plan for people who work after 65? Should benefits be frozen at age 65? Should post-65 employees keep on building up pension credits at the usual rate? Is there some middle course? Or will the government make the decision for us?

In reality, this has turned out to be less of a problem than originally feared. The age for retirement has actually been following a trend in the opposite direction: About four out of five Americans now voluntarily retire *before* age 65. (See Chapter 4 for a further discussion of postretirement benefits.)

What about early retirement?

This brings us to the more critical question of how early retirement will affect an employee's pension. All pension plans have rules stating how much someone receives if he or she decides to retire early (and, of course, is vested). The pension is usually calculated by the plan's standard age-and-service formula—but the monthly amount is then subject to an *actuarial reduction.*

The reason for this reduction is a good one: Someone who retires early can usually look forward to living for a greater number of postretirement years. This means that his or her total lifetime pension money must be divided into a greater number of monthly payments, each of which will be smaller than they would have been if this person had waited until age 65 to retire.

Another complication may arise if someone wants to retire before age 62—when Social Security checks can begin. In order to keep total monthly income the same, the company pension may be larger at the beginning, before Social Security, and then be reduced later on.

On the other hand, if a company, for its own reasons, wants to *encourage* people to take early retirement, it may decide to waive the actuarial reduction and offer employees the option of retiring early at a full pension. (This is sometimes known as opening up a *retirement window.*)

How is a pension paid out?

The first answer to this question would usually be: as a monthly amount for the rest of your life. But, as usual, there are complications. Suppose you have dependents—what happens to them when you die? Most plans offer a number of options to cover this situation. A retiree can sign up for various survivor arrangements, under which, for instance, a husband agrees to receive a smaller pension during his own lifetime in return for a guarantee that payments will continue to his widow if he should die first. There are many variations on this theme, and explaining them to someone about to retire is an important job, since once a payment option is chosen it usually can't be changed. (In fact, the law now requires that a spouse who doesn't want a survivor benefit must state this fact in writing.)

Another payment option, offered by a significant number of plans today, is to receive one lump sum at retirement rather than a series of monthly payments for the rest of one's life. Under present law, this results in some nice tax breaks, such as the "10-year forward averaging" rule and the privilege of rolling over the entire sum into an Individual Retirement Account (IRA). What's more, a lump sum can be very attractive to people who feel they can do better by investing on their own rather than relying on the company's conservative pension managers. (Indeed, if there *is* a lump-sum option in a plan, about three out of four retirees will take advantage of it.) And, of course, the company gets the chance to clear up its books and doesn't have to keep track of a retiree's whereabouts as monthly checks are mailed out for many future years. But there *is* that nagging feeling of responsibility: What do you do if one of your former employees loses his entire lifetime pension money in some ill-advised investment scheme? As one cynic has said, "A lot of the time, with lump sums we're talking Las Vegas."

How is a pension integrated with Social Security?
This is one of those concepts that seems to make a lot of theoretical sense but is very difficult to explain...and to sell. Not too many years ago, when Social Security payments were still quite small, many plans simply ignored Social Security entirely. However, as Social Security benefits—to say nothing of the contributions made by both employers and workers—became much larger, there were complications. Now it was quite possible (at least theoretically) for someone to receive a total income, combining both Social Security and a

generous company pension, that actually was *larger* than what he or she had earned while working. This resulted, to a large extent, because Social Security payments are somewhat distorted to favor low-income workers, who usually receive a monthly benefit that is equal to a larger percentage of their preretirement paycheck.

Thus, many company plans resort to a method of "offsetting" a pension to account for Social Security. One way of doing so is to calculate a retiree's expected primary Social Security benefit and subtract a portion of this benefit in determining the actual monthly payment from the company's plan. (The amount subtracted is often 50 percent, using the logic that employers have been paying 50 percent of Social Security contributions.) Logical as this may be, it's a tough chore to explain it satisfactorily to employees, who may feel that something is being arbitrarily—and unfairly—taken away from them.

A more subtle solution is to build the Social Security offset right into the pension formula itself—by using one pension credit formula up to the salary level covered by Social Security and a more generous formula for any salary above the Social Security base. This, of course, has the advantage of being so complicated that most employees don't really understand what's being done—and thus probably won't complain so loudly. However, it is difficult to control, since the plan's formulas must change every year to keep pace with the annual cost-of-living increases in the Social Security maximum earnings base.

In any case, a number of rather complicated legal restrictions must be followed in integrating a pension plan with Social Security. These have been set up, for the most part, to prevent plans from discriminating against lower-paid employees.

What are the death and disability benefits?
A pension plan usually has provisions to take care of these disasters. Under the law, there must be a "joint and survivor" option covering all employees when they come within 10 years

of normal retirement (usually at age 55). This option means that pension benefits will go to a person's spouse if he or she dies before actually starting to get a pension.

In the rare case where an employee becomes permanently disabled, most pension plans allow normal pension credits to continue to add up, even if the disabled person never returns to work. Then, at retirement age, a pension begins, based on his or her salary before becoming disabled. In most cases, the disability benefit applies to everyone who is covered by the pension plan—even those who are not yet vested.

What about cost-of-living increases for retirees?
This is another controversial subject. Inflation has meant that people who retired years ago on what then seemed to be generous company pensions have, as time has passed, found themselves able to buy less and less.

Unfortunately for them, most pension plans have no provision to take care of the situation. Many companies have made ad hoc increases in pensions, but these increases have depended solely on a particular firm's generosity...or business success. Automatic cost-of-living escalator provisions are virtually nonexistent with private pensions—in sharp contrast, again, with Social Security. And for good reason: Providing them could be extremely expensive (as Social Security has discovered).

MULTI-EMPLOYER PLANS
Until now, we have been concerned only with pension plans sponsored by individual companies for the benefit of their own employees. In a number of industries, however—particularly those with many relatively small firms and a strong labor union—multi-employer retirement systems have been established. (There are also multi-employer plans designed for nonprofit groups, such as the teaching profession's Teachers Insurance Annuity Association.) Each employer contributes to a central pool for the workers on his payroll, funds are managed and invested by a

board of trustees, and benefits are paid out according to established, uniform rules.

These plans have obvious advantages for the small employer, who is responsible only for a fixed per-employee contribution and none of the headaches of running his own pension plan. For the employee, there is the advantage of portability: You don't lose pension credits by moving from one company to another—as long as you stay in the same industry.

ALTERNATIVES TO THE DEFINED-BENEFIT PENSION PLAN

In an attempt to avoid some of the problems presented by a conventional defined-benefit plan—and also to avoid some of the burdens of government rules and regulations—many companies have begun to look elsewhere for an effective retirement program for their employees. And, often, what they have turned to is some sort of *defined-contribution* plan. These plans can take a number of forms: profit-sharing, thrift and savings plans, stock bonus programs, and the new cash or deferred arrangements. Many of these alternatives, of course, have been around for a long time—some, in fact, actually predate the defined-benefit plan idea.

Despite the many differences among these defined-contribution plans, they have one aspect in common: A company decides, according to business conditions or any other consideration, to make a regular contribution to this plan. It recognizes that a host of factors will determine what will happen to this contribution; therefore, there's no guarantee as to what kind of future benefit for retirees (if any at all) will result from this contribution. (A conventional defined-benefit pension plan is almost exactly the reverse: The company decides what kind of pension benefits it wants its retired employees to receive; then it regularly makes the best financial arrangements it can to achieve that goal.)

In the next section ("Other Retirement and Capital Accumulation Programs") we shall discuss many of these alternatives. We shall also compare defined-benefit and defined-contribution plans, describing how each can serve as either a retirement vehicle or a nonretirement vehicle, and also how they differ on such factors as risk, portability, administration, taxes, and the impact on employees.

TERMINATION OF A DEFINED-BENEFIT PENSION PLAN

In the last few years, much publicity has come to an action that could have an explosive impact on the traditional world of employee benefits: deliberate termination of a company's pension plan. Conventionally, a plan termination occurs when its sponsors are in the final throes of financial distress—and the Pension Benefit Guaranty Corporation was set up under ERISA to help protect employees from the ill effects of just such an action.

But this isn't always the case. A financially stable firm may consciously decide that it would be a good business decision to end a defined-benefit plan. The list of those who have done just this in recent years includes such companies as Celanese, Harper & Row, Firestone, Diamond International, Reynolds Metals, and Occidental Petroleum, to name just a few of the largest.

Why would they want to do this? Almost always, because the pension fund represents a huge amount of money—much more than what's needed to provide the plan's promised retirement benefits. So the company may feel it can make much better use of this tempting "excess" financial resource. Other business objectives can seem more worthwhile—at least at the moment—than building up money beyond what is needed for future retirement payments. These might include an expensive expansion program, the acquisition of another company, fighting a takeover attempt, retiring debt—or simply some pressing business difficulty.

For some companies, the amount that has been accumulated to meet future pension obligations actually *is* much larger than it really needs to be. This is a relatively recent problem. No further back than the 1970s or even as late as the early 1980s, it was still common to worry that American pension plans were in deep, deep trouble because they were *under*funded. (And, of course, some still are in real financial difficulty.) For many plans, the stock market boom and high interest rates of 1982 and 1983 led to large increases in their funds' assets. Meanwhile, liabilities were often less than expected, because of greater-than-anticipated employee turnover and layoffs, which meant a smaller bill for pension payments.

Even though a company can quickly adjust to such a situation by reducing its future pension-plan contributions, there's no way it can legally touch money contributed in the past. Under the law, as long as a plan is continued, contributions, once they have been made to a qualified pension plan, may be used only for the benefit of plan members.

However, no law says that a pension plan is immortal; in fact, it can be terminated almost at will. Of course, there are some restrictions. Pensions that have begun for retired employees must be continued, and money that has already been contributed to finance present employees' vested benefits can't be diverted to some other use. But most companies can easily do all that and still have a lot left over—which makes "recovery of excess fund assets" very attractive.

As usual, good arguments can be raised to support either side of this question:

For plan termination. It's the company's money, after all. It isn't the company's fault that conservative financial planning and unexpected developments in the economy led to excess funding. The company took the risk; if things had gone in the opposite direction, it would have had to make up for any underfunding. The cost of a defined-benefit plan can vary widely and unpredictably from year to year. Once the current plan is terminated, it can be replaced by a new one that will be better for everyone than the old plan was—and one that will cost a predictable amount each year.

Against plan termination. It isn't fair to change the rules in the middle of the game. The company *is* at fault for bad planning and pumping too much money into the pension plan, when this could have gone, instead, to other employee benefits or to the company's shareholders. Under a new plan, people close to retirement won't get the pensions they have been expecting. And people who already have retired will never get a cost-of-living increase. It's pension piracy.

If a company *does* go ahead with a termination plan, it must follow certain rules. Pensions for current retirees must be protected, usually by purchasing individual annuities from an insurance company. (However, retirees probably *won't* benefit from any cost-of-living increases in the future.)

The law also says that all active employees covered by the plan must receive the "fair value" of the pension credits they have accumulated, either as some kind of annuity or as a lump-sum payment. And here there's an unexpected break for shorter-term employees. These payments must go to all people covered by the plan that is being terminated, not just those who were already vested.

To replace the plan that is terminated, a company has many choices. It can set up one of the many defined-contribution arrangements discussed in the next section. Or it can restart its old plan, or something very much like it, all over again. Of course, employees may not all benefit in the same way as under the old plan. Some might do better; some might do worse. In fact, if it really wanted to, the company could do nothing at all to replace the old plan.

The whole subject of plan termination and asset revision, however, may soon become academic. Pressure is growing for federal legislation to make recovery of "excess" assets much more difficult. And, if this does occur, it seems likely that defined-benefit pension plans will become even *less* popular—and the dangers of underfunding will increase.

SOME THINGS TO CONSIDER ABOUT PENSION PLANS

What is a company's duty toward employees who retire?

Actually, it has none at all. If a company wants to be tough-minded about it (or has such a young staff that no one really cares) it need do nothing more than make its obligatory Social Security contributions. Most companies will probably want to do more than that, however—even if only to make sure that their own top executives are covered by a qualified pension plan. Pension plans come in an almost infinite variety of combinations and permutations, of which we have only scratched the surface. And the many benefits consultants will be happy to explain them. But a variety of ways to provide money for employees' future security is now available—and some of them don't necessarily follow the lines of the conventional defined-benefit pension plan.

Is the "three-legged stool" concept still valid?
A long-popular image used in connection with retirement income is that of the "three-legged stool." The implication is that the way to survive in retirement is to depend, like a stool, on three supports: Social Security, a private pension, and income from one's own assets. Unfortunately, this is much too simplified to stand up under close inspection. There are just too many variables. Some people will never work long enough at one job to be vested in any kind of a private pension. Some people, no matter how much they want to, may never be able to invest for their own retirement. And some people will be at such a high income level that their Social Security check becomes relatively meaningless. On the other hand, there will always be *some* people who'll make use of all three types of resources—although how much they benefit from each of them will vary greatly.

How will demographic changes affect pension plans?
One problem with many pension plans (like many other employee benefits) is that they were established in the days of the conventional family unit—male breadwinner who spent most of his life working for the same company with a wife at home taking care of their two children. That was probably a misconception to begin with, but it goes without saying that this conventional family is becoming an endangered species today. And pension plans, if they are going to work as planned, must

do something for the increasing number of women in the work force—who are much less likely to spend an uninterrupted lifetime career with one company. In particular, it would seem about time to take a fresh look at vesting requirements. What does a plan with a 10-year vesting requirement offer to people who change jobs so often that they never stay 10 years in one place?

Are lump-sum payments a good idea?

Although a growing number of defined-benefit pension plans are offering lump-sum payments to retirees, companies might well take a second look at this practice—especially if they also have defined-contribution arrangements that will pay off in a lump sum. The rationale for having a pension plan in the first place is to provide a guaranteed *lifetime* income for retiring employees. *Retirees* may truly believe that they can take a lump sum, invest it privately, and achieve better results for themselves than the company's pension can—but the odds are against it.

Is the conventional defined-benefit plan outmoded?

We have pointed out some valid reasons why the current trend away from the traditional kind of annuity pension arrangement has developed. Many companies may agree, and look elsewhere—especially if they are just getting started. However, this shouldn't necessarily imply that the defined-benefit plan has seen its day. It still has definite points in its favor.

Actually, the most practical solution for many companies may be to use *both* kinds of retirement arrangements. One solution is to have a conventional defined-benefit pension plan as a floor to provide a relatively modest retirement benefit (but a guaranteed one) to all long-service employees, with a defined-contribution arrangement built on top of this floor, which will (with good fortune) provide something for everyone. And benefits consultants are now diligently at work devising ingenious combinations of the defined-benefit and defined-contribution concepts, such as "cash account" or "cash balance" pension plans which provide both a promise of long-term benefits *and* a growing cash balance.

Should a pension plan ever be terminated?
We have listed the pros and cons above; the final decision is up to the individual company. But no one should expect a plan termination to be easy. As always, many employees will complain vehemently at the very hint of anything that appears to be a cutback in their benefits—even if they actually will be better off in the long run. Needless to say, the more attractive the new plan is made to be, the less will be the employee resistance to getting rid of the old one.

Can we expect future legislation on pension plans?
Certainly. We've already seen a lot of it, and there's no reason to believe that the government will stop paying attention to the country's aging—and increasingly vocal—population.

To Sum Up
- Pension plans are unique among employee benefits. To some employees, a company's pension plan is the most important of all benefits; to others, it ranks almost at the very bottom on the scale of importance.
- The defined-benefit annuity pension plan, long the traditional arrangement, is undergoing an agonizing reappraisal. In many cases, it originated in a time when the demographic makeup of many companies' employee populations was quite different from what it is today.
- As a result, a growing number of companies may be tempted to terminate their traditional plans and substitute some much different arrangement, probably a defined-contribution plan of some sort. Many more, not wanting to take such a drastic step, may well consider freezing their present pension plans where they now are, and making any future improvements in other directions. And still others will be restructuring their defined-benefit plans to accommodate a changing work force.

- In any case, if a company has not taken a long, hard look at its pension plan in recent months it would be very well advised to do so.

OTHER RETIREMENT AND CAPITAL-ACCUMULATION PROGRAMS

As we explained in the previous section, increasing attention is being paid to some interesting alternatives to the conventional pension plan. This section deals with many of them. We shall discuss traditional profit-sharing plans, stock ownership plans, thrift and savings plans, and the new cash-or-deferred arrangements—also known as Section 401[k] plans. To complete the retirement-income picture, we have also included a brief discussion of Social Security's retirement benefits. Finally, one other aspect of retirement: the preretirement programs that many companies have established for employees who are approaching that often-traumatic milestone.

PROFIT-SHARING PLANS

Profit sharing is a well-established idea. More than a hundred years ago, such companies as General Foods and Pillsbury Mills were giving a percentage of their net profits to employees as an extra bonus. And the first deferred profit-sharing plan was developed by the Harris Trust & Savings Bank in Chicago as long ago as 1916. But, like so many other employee benefits, profit sharing came into its own during World War II, because of the freeze on regular wage increases. Additional impetus came after the passage of ERISA in 1974, since small companies often found that a simple profit-sharing plan avoided the many rules and regulations associated with a pension plan. Today, it's estimated that almost one-third of all

American corporations share their profits with their employees in some way.

HOW THEY WORK
The basic reason for a profit-sharing plan couldn't be simpler: When a company has a good year and makes a profit, it's only fair that part of this profit should go to the employees who helped achieve it; this will encourage them to continue the good work in the future. For the company, there's no ironclad obligation. If it *isn't* a good year, no contribution need be made. In years when the company does contribute a portion of its profits, the mathematics are relatively easy: Calculate exactly how much of the profit is to be shared, and divide it up among employees, usually according to some simple formula based on salary.

Cash or deferred?
Sometimes employees will receive their full share of the profits as cash at the end of the year. This has the advantage of being immediately recognizable and appreciated as a genuine company benefit. But it has the distinct disadvantage of being taxable as ordinary income—so that income tax is usually withheld from the profit-sharing check before the employee even sees it. Some companies may prefer to translate the cash bonus into shares of company stock, as a more meaningful bonus—but the same tax rules apply.

It's much more common, therefore, for a company to institute a *deferred* profit-sharing plan that has been qualified by the Internal Revenue Service. Under the law, benefits from this kind of plan aren't taxable until they are actually received—and, meanwhile, the full amount can be invested and, with luck, grow.

A third possibility is to combine the cash and deferred ideas—offering employees the opportunity to take a portion of their share in cash and have the balance placed in their deferred account. This decision usually is irrevocable; any money that isn't taken as cash is treated the same as all other deferred money.

The size of the contribution

A profit-sharing plan usually will include a set formula—based on a company's net profit, earnings growth, return on equity, or whatever—that determines the size of its annual contribution to the profit-sharing pool. Or the board of directors will simply make a business judgment each year as to how much the company can afford to contribute.

This sum can then be translated into a percentage of the company's total payroll—and each eligible employee's account will receive the same percentage of his or her annual pay. Under the tax law, the annual limit on this percentage is 15 percent of salary, but if a company contributes less than 15 percent in one year, the difference can be carried over to a following year (subject to an overall maximum of 25 percent a year).

Some companies may use a sliding formula, with different percentages being awarded according to length of service. There also may be fairly strict limitations on which employees share in the profits—there could, for instance, be a waiting period or one, two, or three years.

Limitations on profit sharing

One important limitation—necessary to gain qualified status for a deferred profit-sharing plan—is that the money in an employee's account not be readily accessible. In fact, the employee may not have any rights to it at all until a vesting period has passed, although this is usually more liberal than the common 10-year period for pension plans. Vesting, however, is a little more complicated to explain with this sort of plan, since, under one common practice, only a portion of the total amount in an account becomes fully vested each year.

Even when it is fully vested, however, an account balance is usually only payable at retirement, death, permanent disability, or termination of employment. Not all plans operate under such strict rules, however. It sometimes is possible for an employee to take out a loan against a vested account balance—or even to make an actual withdrawal—but often with rather strict rules that limit such loans and withdrawals to genuine emergencies.

Investment choices
Employees' profit-sharing accounts may consist of a single company-managed investment fund or be allocated to a choice of different funds—company stock, fixed-income securities, growth stocks, etc. If there's more than one fund, employees usually have the chance to apportion their accounts among the various investment opportunities and to shift money from one fund to another at specified times. Earnings from all the funds are usually reinvested, and accounts that are forfeited by employees who leave before becoming vested are distributed among the remaining accounts.

SOME THINGS TO CONSIDER ABOUT PROFIT SHARING
Does it really increase productivity?
The original thinking behind the profit-sharing concept was to encourage employees to work harder and more effectively to achieve the business success that would increase their company's profits—which they would then share. It's still a fine idea, but, unfortunately, not a very practical one in today's world. Except in very small companies—and for the top echelon of policy-making executives in larger ones—the individual employee today can only have, at best, a minuscule effect on company profits. Nevertheless, a profit-sharing plan may achieve less tangible results—such as greater employee morale and an increased identification with a company's business objectives.

Can a profit-sharing plan be effective as a pension plan?
Many firms establish profit-sharing plans for the express purpose of providing retirement income for their employees. However, this goal is difficult to achieve—especially if the prime objective is to provide a guaranteed lifetime income to retired employees. For a long-term employee, a profit-sharing

plan resembles the *career-average* type of pension plan, and thus cannot produce a pension based on final average pay. Of course, with exceptional investment results, a profit-sharing plan might build up account balances for employees that would yield even more than would a final-pay pension plan. But that can't ever be guaranteed in advance. With bad luck, an employee might happen to retire just when the company's profit-sharing investments were at an all-time low point. Also, there is no very practical way for a profit-sharing plan to be integrated with Social Security.

Are employees prepared for the risks?
It can be a shattering experience for employees, particularly those who are unaware of the risks of financial investments, to see their cherished profit-sharing account balances take a sudden nosedive. It's important that all participants in a plan be well-informed about the risks involved, particularly if they are going to be responsible for making choices among a variety of funds.

Will they begin to take things for granted?
That can be a real danger with a long-established profit-sharing plan. Employees will begin to count on their annual profit-sharing allotments as an expected part of pay and be very upset if they don't get them. Ironically, this is more likely with the most successful plans. If you've been getting a regular profit-sharing check equal to, say, 15 percent of your salary every year, it's only natural to be less than happy in a year when that check is only 9 percent.

Is portability always an advantage?
The fact that a profit-sharing account will become vested very rapidly—if not immediately—makes it attractive to younger, short-term employees. It's one benefit they can be sure of getting sooner or later. But this very characteristic may actually have a negative effect: A successful middle manager who has built up a handsome balance in a profit-sharing account may be strongly tempted to leave—and get hold of that balance im-

mediately. (That's one reason why extremely strict prohibitions against loans and withdrawals may sometimes be ill-advised.)

STOCK-OWNERSHIP PLANS

Like profit sharing, the idea of having employees own shares of stock in their company has a certain appeal. Two kinds of plans are now available to companies who would like to use stock ownership to give employees a feeling of genuine participation in their company's success (assuming it is successful). For some reason, all plans of this kind get to be known by acronyms; we shall discuss here both the PAYSOP (payroll-based stock-ownership plan) and the ESOP (employee stock ownership plan).

PAYSOPs

The PAYSOP concept first went into effect in 1983 and, unless its life is extended by the government, will be available for only a limited period. It replaced an earlier version, the TRASOP (Tax Reduction Act stock-ownership plan), which was in existence from 1975 to 1983. With a PAYSOP, a company may choose to make an annual tax-deductible allocation of shares of its stock to its employees. However, the stock that can be awarded in this way is quite limited: The maximum amount can only be equal to half of one percent of an employee's annual pay up to $100,000. (Originally, this percentage had been scheduled to rise to three-quarters of one percent in 1985, but the 1984 tax law froze the figure at the half-of-one-percent level.)

Under a PAYSOP, someone earning $32,000 could receive shares of stock with a market value of $160—or five shares if the company's stock were worth $32 a share—and someone making more than $100,000 a year, using the same example, would get $500 worth of stock. These shares aren't immediately available—and they won't be until seven years have elapsed; only then is an employee entitled to his or her shares (or their cash value at the time). Meanwhile, all employee shares are held by the company, and dividends, if any, will accumulate. No tax is due, of course, until the shares are actually received.

The value of the stock is also payable at retirement or death, and the PAYSOP must have rules to cover what happens to shares held in the names of people who leave the company.

ESOPs

Although it's similar in many ways to a PAYSOP, an employee stock ownership plan differs in a number of important aspects. The ESOP concept has been around for more than 50 years; in fact, a limited number of companies (most of them relatively small) have been using these plans to serve as a kind of defined-contribution retirement plan. Over the years, employees can accumulate a substantial number of shares of stock in their company, rather than a cash balance.

As far as employees are concerned, the allotment of stock can be considerably greater than under a PAYSOP—but the ground rules are somewhat stricter. The upper limit for an employee's ESOP allocation is 25 percent of annual pay. However, if the company also has another kind of pension plan, the total contribution for both it and the ESOP is also 25 percent (with a provision for carryovers from previous years).

Active employees can't get their hands on any of the stock they may receive from an ESOP. Shares and accumulated earnings are paid out at retirement or death, and, of course, the plan will establish vesting rules for people who leave early. Under these, as in other plans, it's very possible that employees who leave with less than 10 years of service may forfeit their entire share allotment.

In recent years, the *leveraged ESOP* idea has gained some popularity. This is a rather complicated arrangement under which the ESOP can serve as a financing vehicle for a company. To establish this kind of plan (with the approval of the Internal Revenue Service), the first step is to set up a trust fund. This trust then uses the company's credit to arrange a loan, with which the company buys a block of its own stock at market value (with the stock serving as collateral for the loan). The company then begins to make annual contributions to the ESOP—each being a partial repayment of the loan. And, as the loan is repaid, a portion of the stock that had been serving as collateral is distributed to company employees. While all this is going on, of course, the company can use—for whatever business purposes it had in mind—the money it received for its stock.

SOME THINGS TO CONSIDER ABOUT STOCK-OWNERSHIP PLANS
Why aren't these plans more popular?
In the first place, PAYSOPs have only been in existence for a few years, so it's not too surprising that they have seen only limited application. Most companies with well-established employee benefit programs, after all, are often slow to adopt entirely new kinds of benefits. Nevertheless, PAYSOPs have been spreading rather rapidly, since they seem to offer an almost foolproof way to give employees a small—but tax-deductible—share in their company. Surprisingly enough, the relatively limited number of shares each person receives doesn't seem to make very much difference—it's the idea that counts.

On the other hand, ESOPs have had a rather bad press over the years. Labor unions, in particular, have always viewed them with skepticism. This may be because an ESOP is seen to be simply a scheme for raising capital in a rather complicated manner—with the employees only a necessary afterthought. However, despite these problems, the numbers of ESOPs have increased considerably in recent years.

Can an ESOP be an effective pension plan?
Although ESOPs do fall under the government's broad definition of a retirement plan, the answer would probably have to

be no—except for a limited number of very fast-growing young companies, whose stock seems destined to increase substantially over the years. In most other cases, ESOPs have the built-in disadvantages of other capital-accumulation arrangements when used as pension plans: They actually are career-average plans, with credits based on earnings over many years rather than final pay; they can't be integrated with Social Security; and, worst of all, their value at retirement is totally unpredictable. In addition, an ESOP has one other strong negative feature: It's putting all your eggs in one basket, since the entire pension fund, under an ESOP, is invested in one company's stock. This problem can be even worse, too, for a small, unlisted company for which the "fair market value" of its stock may be difficult to determine.

THRIFT AND SAVINGS PLANS

These plans appear under a variety of names: thrift plans, savings plans, investment plans, thrift investment plans, savings investment plans, and so forth. Whatever the title, they all have one common feature: Both employees and the company make contributions to them. This means, then, that these plans are really hybrids, since different sets of rules apply to the two kinds of contributions.

For the employee, any of these plans usually is a very good deal. In fact, when such a plan is established, a company will find, more often than not, that a substantial majority of its employees will decide to join—and save the maximum amount allowed under the plan. And why not? Where else can you get, say, a guaranteed 50 percent return on your investment each year?

Note: In this section we are only discussing conventional thrift and savings plans, to which employees contribute after-tax money; plans in which it is possible to contribute pretax dollars—the so-called 401[k] plans—are covered in the next section.

HOW THEY WORK

The basic principle involved here is that of matching. Employees decide to contribute a certain percentage of their pay to the plan and this amount is matched by a contribution from their employer. For the employee, it is usually an even percentage of salary—1, 2, 3 percent...up to a maximum of 6 percent, which is the most the law allows to be matched (under the theory that permitting any more would be discriminatory in favor of higher-paid workers, who would be the only ones who could afford that much).

No fixed rules govern the size of the employer's matching contribution. Most often, it's half that of the employee. In other words, if you contribute 6 percent of your pay, your company will match it with an amount equal to 3 percent. The contribution can be more or less than half—in some cases, a company may even make a dollar-for-dollar match. And a company may change its matching percentage from year to year—according to its business success, perhaps. Another option is to have a sliding scale of matching percentages, with different ratios being used according to an employee's length of service or earnings bracket.

Many plans also permit employees to add on an extra contribution above the amount that the company matches simply to take advantage of the investment opportunities offered by the savings plan. Thus, using the example above, an employee might decide to contribute 10 percent of pay into the thrift plan, but the company would still match only the first 6 percent—for a total contribution of 13 percent (10 percent from the employee plus 3 percent from the employer).

Almost always, of course, employee contributions are through payroll deductions, which provide the advantage of virtually painless savings—as in the long-established payroll savings and U.S. Savings Bond plans. And some plans offer the opportunity for as much as $2,000 of each employee's annual contribution to be designated as a tax-free IRA deduction.

As in a profit-sharing plan, a thrift or savings plan will usually offer a choice of investment funds—perhaps company stock, a conservative fixed-income fund, some investments with greater growth potential (and risk), etc. And it's possible to move investments from one fund to another—and, within limits, change the percentage of contribution.

A company's thrift/savings plan contribution must follow many of the same ground rules as those for the conventional profit-sharing plans discussed earlier. Vesting rules are also similar. The full company contribution, plus any earnings, is usually payable only at retirement, death, or termination of employment. Several vesting rules apply to employees who leave early, and other provisions cover withdrawals or loans; these often are restricted to genuine emergencies.

However, for the portion of each account that represents an employee's own contribution an entirely different set of rules is in effect. This money is always completely vested—and the rules on withdrawals are more liberal. But a thrift plan isn't supposed to serve as a savings account, and most companies place limits on the amount of in-and-out activity an employee can engage in, even if it is his or her own money. One expanded version of the thrift/savings plan concept combines it with a profit-sharing plan: The company makes an annual contribution to employees' accounts from its profits and also agrees to match employee contributions. Here, all the company's contributions—both profit sharing and matching—would be treated by one set of rules, while more liberal provisions would apply to the portion of the account that came from the employee's own contributions. (However, many plans of this kind are now being replaced by the 401[k] plans discussed below.)

SOME THINGS TO CONSIDER ABOUT THRIFT/SAVINGS PLANS
Is there a danger of overselling a plan like this?
As we have explained, an obvious advantage of a thrift plan is the very generous return on an employee's investment in the year in which it is made—perhaps in the neighborhood of 50 percent. However, everyone must understand that no in-

vestments are free of risk. An employee who chooses to put his or her savings into an investment fund that is composed largely of common stocks, for example, must recognize that the stock market goes both up and down—and be prepared for the bad news that will inevitably occur in some years.

What about replacing profit sharing with a thrift plan?
A company with a long-established pure profit-sharing arrangement—one that paid out cash at the end of each year—might decide, for perfectly good business reasons, to replace it with a thrift/savings plan. But employees may not greet the change with joy. No matter how generous the terms of this new plan, many employees will resent having, for the first time, to contribute some of their own money.

CASH-OR-DEFERRED ARRANGEMENTS

We come now to a very popular kind of plan—the talk of the benefits business in recent years. Most properly, it should go under the name of *cash-or-deferred arrangement (CODA)*, but it has become known much more familiarly as a *401[k] plan*—taking the name from a section of the Internal Revenue Code that was added by the Revenue Act of 1978. (The big move toward establishing plans of this kind didn't come, however, until final regulations were issued in 1982.)

When these plans first became popular, they were sometimes called *salary-reduction plans*—a most unfortunate and misleading title, since no one's salary is really "reduced" in the usual meaning of that word. It's no great surprise that this designation, with all its negative implications, has begun to disappear. But, whatever names they may go by, these plans are certainly gaining widespread favor; according to one survey, more than three-quarters of the country's larger firms had adopted 401[k] plans by 1986. Many of these, of course, were not entirely new benefits, but were simply established thrift/savings plans that had been modified to fit under the 401[k] umbrella.

In essence, 401[k] plans are very similar to the profit-sharing and thrift plans we have discussed previously—with some significant tax-saving features that are particularly attractive to higher-paid employees. (And this, of course, may be one reason why they have suddenly received so much attention.)

HOW THEY WORK
As profit-sharing plans
In this new twist on the conventional profit-sharing arrangement, the company's contribution is made in the usual way, but each employee must decide whether to have the entire amount placed into an investment account ("deferred") or to receive a portion of it immediately in cash. Often, the plan requires that a minimum percentage—say 50 percent—must be deferred. (Here, and in many other respects, this kind of plan is virtually identical to conventional profit-sharing plans; the chief difference is in the new tax provisions.)

As thrift plans
In a technical sense, these really are "salary reduction plans," for they allow employees to reduce their *taxable* income by making contributions to thrift or savings plans like the ones described in the previous section. Employees don't see this money; it's taken right off the top of their pay. These before-tax contributions are usually matched by a company contribution, based on one of the formulas already described. In actual fact, there need not be any company contribution, but plans of this kind are, understandably, not too well received by most employees.

Some plans also make it possible for employees to make additional *after*-tax contributions to the plan; these may be matched, or they may not be. In almost all other respects—investment options, withdrawals, loans, vesting rules, payment methods—a plan qualified under Section 401[k] can be set up to closely resemble a conventional thrift plan.

Tax advantages under section 401[k]

Just what *are* the tax-saving provisions of 401[k]? First, as we have explained, any before-tax money that an employee chooses to contribute to one of these plans actually does "reduce" his or her salary for income tax purposes (although it is still subject to Social Security taxes). But, as usual, there's no free lunch. When an employee eventually receives this money, plus whatever it may have earned in the meantime, it's all taxable as ordinary income.

There's another tax break under Section 401[k]. Under present law, when you receive a lump sum from one of these qualified plans, you may use the *10-year forward averaging method* to calculate the income tax due on it. And, especially for someone in a higher tax bracket, this can amount to a substantial saving, since investment earnings may be spread over a 10-year period, rather than being taxable all at once.

SOME THINGS TO CONSIDER ABOUT CASH-OR-DEFERRED ARRANGEMENTS
How do these plans compare with IRAs?

That's a question employees frequently ask. In the very first place, there's no reason—as long as someone can afford it—not to invest in one of these plans and an Individual Retirement Account; both offer ways in which people can reduce their taxable incomes. But, assuming there must be a choice, these are some points to consider:

- There's no matching feature in an IRA; all the money must come from your own pocket.
- An IRA has a $2,000 annual limit on contributions; with a Section 401[k] plan, the limit is 20 percent of pay, up to a maximum contribution of $30,000 per year under the original law (with this maximum subject to possible reduction under proposed tax laws).
- You may contribute to a 401[k] in small amounts deducted from each paycheck; there's never a required lump-sum deposit, as in some IRAs.

- Under an IRA, there's a 10 percent penalty for withdrawing money before age 59 1/2; this doesn't apply to the new plans (although there are some restrictions on when withdrawals may be made).
- Under many of the 401[k] plans, it's possible to borrow from the balance in your account and then repay the loan (to yourself) under easy terms; this can't be done with an IRA.
- And, finally, the 10-year averaging method can't be used in calculating the tax on a lump-sum payment from an IRA.

What about "discrimination"?
At the beginning of the 401[k] boom, many people were fearful that special regulations, designed to prevent discrimination in favor of the highest-paid one-third of a company's employees, might present difficult problems. This has turned out to be a false alarm, however, since workable techniques to prevent charges of discrimination have been developed. And, what's more, 401[k] plans have turned out to be more popular with the "lower two-thirds" than many people thought they would be—with 70, 80, or even 100 percent participation being relatively common.

DEFINED-BENEFIT PLANS VS. DEFINED-CONTRIBUTION PLANS

Many companies may want to consider adopting one of the defined-contribution plans we have been discussing in this chapter instead of a conventional defined-benefit pension plan—or, more likely, as a supplement to such a plan. But, before doing so, it must be clearly understood that there are some fundamental differences between the two. In the following comparison, we shall explain the areas in which they differ (sometimes referring, for simplicity, to the two alternatives as "pension plans" and "contribution plans," rather than "defined-benefit plans" and "defined-contribution plans").

As a retirement benefit

A conventional defined-benefit pension plan usually will be more attractive to older employees who are nearing retirement and to those who have already accumulated a fairly long period of service with a company, since it puts heavy emphasis on years of past service and offers very predictable retirement benefits.

A defined-contribution plan, by contrast, usually makes little or no allowance for past service. Future benefits from this kind of plan are much less predictable. Also, once an employee has retired, a pension plan will pay a guaranteed life income. But, even when a contribution plan is intended to be part of a company's retirement program, an employee must make his or her own investments after retirement—with no guarantees that these will produce a satisfactory lifetime income.

As a nonretirement benefit

To get funds from a defined-benefit pension plan, even if it has a lump-sum provision, an employee must cease active work for a company, in one way or another. However, someone can remain eligible for a vested pension from one company (or even start getting it under early retirement), but now be actively at work somewhere else.

When they were originally conceived, defined-contribution plans were not usually thought of as retirement vehicles. Instead, most of them were designed to provide convenient ways for employees to save and invest for their future—not just for retirement. Vesting requirements are usually more liberal, and funds often are available for use when they are needed for special purposes.

Risk

In a traditional defined-benefit pension plan, the company takes the investment risk. It commits itself to a specific financial objective, and, if its funding arrangements and investment decisions don't do as well as hoped, it is the company that must bear the financial burden.

In a defined-contribution plan, it's quite the opposite. The employee takes the risk. The company contributes what it can afford—not what it must—each year. Employees have to wait and see what happens to this money. Sometimes they can share in the decisions as to how it is invested; sometimes they can't. And a history of poor investments can leave them, literally, with nothing at all in the plan.

Portability

In a conventional defined-benefit pension plan, as we have explained, if you aren't vested—and it's usually 10 years before you are—you get nothing at all if you leave a company. And, even if you *are* vested, you usually must wait until you're 65 years old to get the full pension you have earned.

Here's where a contribution plan is much more attractive to today's frequent job-changer. Vesting almost always occurs sooner than under a pension plan; with some contribution plans it even may be full and immediate. If you change jobs, you'll certainly get back your own contributions and any earnings; it's quite likely you'll get your company's contributions also. And these are yours to invest or spend immediately.

Administration

A pension plan involves actuarial calculations, investment decisions, government reporting requirements, and contributions to the Pension Benefit Guaranty Corporation. In short, many *long-term* commitments. But, on a day-to-day basis, the only administrative problems are to calculate and begin paying individual pensions as they come due.

Contribution plans, although basically simpler in design, can involve a good deal of ongoing record-keeping, because of the regular stream of deposits and withdrawals, although there is considerably less government regulation and reporting. However, regular calculations of the status of individual accounts must be undertaken and reported to employees—often on a quarterly basis.

Taxes

For a pension plan, the tax situation is fairly straightforward: Under present law, the employer can deduct its contributions to the plan as a business expense; an employee doesn't pay taxes until benefits start coming in.

Contribution plans, however, present a variety of tax situations, as we have explained in this chapter. They can involve both pretax and after-tax contributions, and benefits can be treated as either regular income or a long-term investment.

Impact on employees

A pension plan is always difficult to explain. It involves complicated formulas, Social Security integration, and the unpredictability of future wages. And only employees with fairly long service and who are beginning to think about retirement will really appreciate its benefits. To them, it will be an extremely important company benefit. For the younger employee, however, the company's pension plan is usually a matter of monumental noninterest.

But a contribution plan—almost any contribution plan—has an immediate impact on everyone who receives benefits from it.

SOCIAL SECURITY

If this book had been written only a few years earlier, it would have been essential to include a detailed discussion of the terrible problems that lay ahead of this country's retiring population because of the impending bankruptcy of the Social Security system. But the panic seems to have subsided. The changes that became effective in 1983—relatively minor though they really were—should have quieted most fears of a Social Security disaster in the near future.

No survey of retirement benefits would be complete without including a brief mention of Social Security. It is, after all, a vital factor in ensuring the financial stability of a great many—perhaps the majority—of Americans.

As we explained earlier, for many people who retire, Social Security may be the *only* source of income; others, with handsome returns from their company pension or private investments—or both—will not place much reliance on their Social Security checks. In fact, it might be better to think of Social Security as a common floor supporting everyone's retirement.

THE RISE OF SOCIAL SECURITY
The early years
Social Security—or, more properly, the Old Age, Survivors, and Disability Insurance Program—has expanded far beyond its relatively modest beginnings in 1935. It's a little difficult to realize today how controversial an innovation it actually was. Until Social Security was initiated in the depths of the Depression, no government-sponsored retirement program existed in this country.

At its start, Social Security was simply a means of providing support to workers and their families upon retirement or to the workers' families in the event of their death ("old age and survivors" insurance). It has since expanded to include other kinds of insurance—for disability and for health (Medicare)—that have created actual and potential financial problems for the system.

The situation today
The contributions received, from both employees and their employers, and the benefits paid out have increased tremendously since the program's inception. In fact, until 1950 the maximum contribution for both employees and employers was one percent of the first $3,000 of annual wages—or a total yearly deduction of $30 each. However, by 1986 this almost-unnoticed $30 annual contribution had risen to a very noticeable one of more than $3,000 from both employee and employer. Benefits have not gone up so spectacularly, but the increase is impressive nevertheless.

Even with the adjustments in the 1983 amendments, the maximum monthly benefit for an individual is now well over $700; in 1954 it was only $85 a month.

However, these figures don't tell the whole story. People who paid the modest contributions of the 1940s, 1950s, and 1960s—and then retired—are today getting the much more generous benefits of the 1980s. For example, take a man who was born in 1905 and had been covered to the maximum extent by the Social Security program from its beginnings until 1970, when he retired at age 65. During the *entire period* from 1937 until 1970 the total amount he contributed to Social Security would have been less than $3,800—plus an equal amount from his employers during that time. But now he and his wife (assuming she is also over 65 and isn't eligible for benefits in her own right) are receiving a *monthly* check of approximately $900—which will continue to go up with the rising cost of living. In other words, *every year* they get back considerably more money than was contributed in his behalf during his entire working career.

One result of the surging growth of the Social Security system is that it has finally become a virtually universal national retirement program. By 1983, it covered approximately 94 percent of American workers, and, with the addition of the federal government and nonprofit employees who were absorbed under the 1983 changes, that figure could approach 100 percent before too long.

Both benefits and maximum taxable earnings are now tied directly into the cost of living, and the contribution rate is scheduled to rise only a fraction of a percent from its present level—to 7.65 percent in 1990 and thereafter. If all goes according to plan, we probably have seen the end of burdensome year-to-year increases in many workers' Social Security withholding.

What about the future?
During the early 1980s, examples like the one of the hypothetical worker above—plus some extremely pessimistic actuarial forecasts—were enough to create a near panic about

the imminent bankruptcy of the entire Social Security program. However, for once something was done about it. A bipartisan national commission was appointed, studied the situation thoroughly, and recommended a number of reforms that, fortunately, were adopted almost without change by the Congress in 1983.

And now, remarkably, the outlook is optimistic. Although some people remain disturbed about Social Security's future, the consensus of informed opinion seems to be that—at least as far as Old Age and Survivors Insurance is concerned—Social Security is pretty well under control. A few problems may occur in the immediate future (up to about 1988), especially if the economy turns downward, but it appears that the program will then be on a secure financial basis from 1988 until 2020. Then, after the baby boomers have retired, there may be a whole new set of problems.

In any case, the political power of the country's elderly population will certainly have increased substantially by that time. And it seems inconceivable that whoever is running the government in 2021 won't be forced to find the appropriate solutions to whatever unexpected problems may have arisen.

SOME THINGS TO CONSIDER ABOUT SOCIAL SECURITY
Just what is it supposed to be, anyway?
The basic philosophy behind the whole idea of Old Age, Survivors, and Disability Insurance has recently been questioned by a number of critics. Is it really an "insurance" program, as its name—and the common insurance terminology it uses—would seem to imply?

Social Security's rather unusual pay-as-you-go financing arrangement does make it radically different from most forms of insurance. But, since benefits are paid out when an uncertain event occurs (for example, when someone lives long enough to retire), it really *is* insurance of a kind. And, as happens with other kinds of insurance, some people may get much more in benefits than they ever paid in—the man we described above, for example. And other people will never even get back what they have contributed over the years (such as someone with no dependents who dies while still actively at work). These inequalities occur with all insurance; yet they still seem to bother some people—the same people, ironically, who may have willingly paid their automobile insurance year after year without ever filing an accident claim.

On the other hand, it's sometimes been suggested that, if Social Security is truly insurance against the perils of retirement, then only those people who really need the benefits should get them. However, the idea of having some kind of "means test" for Social Security has never been very popular—especially with those who have been contributing a lot of money to the program over the years. But the 1983 amendments did include one small step in this direction: for the first time, Social Security payments are now considered taxable income to retired people with incomes above a certain level.

Are more changes needed?
Although the 1983 amendments did make some significant changes that may well assure the program's financial health into the next century, they didn't solve everything. In particular, Social Security was set up in the days of the traditional family—in most cases, a male wage earner with a nonworking wife. As a result, many of its provisions don't seem totally fair to such widespread latter-day institutions as working women and two-earner families. Why, for instance, should a wife who has worked most of her life at relatively modest pay (making Social Security contributions all the time) get no more when she retires than a housewife who has never paid Social Security but is automatically entitled to a check equal to half her husband's benefit?

This, and other apparent inequalities in the treatment of the sexes, may mean that the greatest pressures for further changes in Social Security will come in that area.

What about financing?

Some other proposed changes revolve around the program's financing arrangements. Should Social Security be supported—at least in part—out of the government's general revenues, rather than relying entirely on pay-as-you-go? (One backdoor method of doing this would be to make Social Security contributions tax deductible to the employee, as they are for the employer.)

Although general-revenue financing may eventually be the only way to solve Medicare's fast-growing financial problems, the 1983 amendments would seem to make this unnecessary for the rest of Social Security. In fact, a reverse problem might occur if the Old Age and Survivors fund goes well into the black in the near future. A big, fat surplus (as such there well may be) might be a tempting possibility for solving some other government agency's temporary financial distress.

What's sacred about age 65?

Nothing, apparently. Although this was the normal retirement age built into Social Security's original charter—and, subsequently, that of most private pension plans—the Age Discrimination in Employment Act has eliminated most compulsory retirement at this age. Now, under the 1983 amendments, the age for receiving full benefits will very gradually move up—beginning in the year 2000. (It will be at age 67 by 2022.) However, since the actual trend has been for people to retire, more often than not, before reaching age 65, we may well see future pressure against ever putting this scheduled change into effect.

PRETIREMENT PLANNING PROGRAMS

Despite all the interesting—and sometimes very lucrative—benefits we have described in this section and the previous one on pensions, retirement itself can still be a traumatic experience for many people. And, with today's longer life expectancies and earlier retirement ages, a person's retirement years can be a fairly long and significant portion of a total life—not just a few last days spent sitting in the sunset.

As a result, many companies have turned their attention to preparing people for retirement, rather than simply giving them a final handshake and opening the door.

HOW THEY WORK

Preretirement programs can take a number of forms. They can be group seminars or individual one-on-one sessions. They can be programs developed by a company to fit its own special situation, or prepackaged sessions prepared by outside consultants. They can be held on company premises or elsewhere. They can last a day or two, or be spread out over a much longer period of time. They can begin just before retirement or much sooner—in some cases, as early as age 55. And they may include the prospective retiree's spouse. But they are almost always voluntary.

What preretirement programs cover

Most preretirement programs are concerned only with financial planning—including, typically, such topics as continuing company benefits, survivor protection, writing a will, investments, how to deal with inflation, estate planning, and taxes. Even in the more elaborate programs, financial problems will often take up at least 60 percent of the time. But a full-scale program also may include such topics as:

- Health—Medicare benefits, nutrition, exercise, physical fitness
- Living arrangements—buying and selling a home, handling a move, information about retirement communities
- New careers—starting a business, temporary employment, volunteer work, Social Security's earnings limitations
- Interpersonal concerns—psychological adjustment to retirement, relationships with family members and friends, company programs such as clubs and newsletters for retirees

- Leisure time—recreation, hobbies, community involvement, continuing education

Whatever their specific content may be, these programs have other virtues besides helping a retiree overcome an often difficult hurdle. They also can provide assistance in the period just before retirement. This can be a time of unusual stress, sometimes beginning several years before an impending retirement, when an aging worker's productivity and general usefulness to the organization may decline.

Preretirement programs also can prevent people from falling into the dangerous habit of entitlement—of feeling they now have been put out to pasture and must rely on gifts from others. Instead, a program can build up the idea of self-reliance and even, perhaps, the start of many productive future years of accomplishment.

To Sum Up

- Today, there are many additional programs that can provide income after retirement—profit sharing, stock ownership, thrift and savings plans, cash-or-deferred arrangements. Many of these can also serve as capital-accumulation methods that can provide substantial returns.
- Although they are receiving much attention right now, some programs (particularly the new Section 401[k] plans) are not, in truth, employee *benefits* in the traditional sense, since most of the impetus behind them comes from their potential tax advantages more than anything else.
- Social Security's problems seem to be solved—at least until well into the twenty-first century—and, more than ever, it will be an important retirement benefit for almost everyone.
- Preretirement programs are a relatively easy and inexpensive method of protecting employees against the potential trauma associated with retirement.

SPECIAL SERVICES

The preceding seven sections of Chapter 2 have described the employee benefits most frequently offered today. We have explained the special features of each type of benefit and considered some of the questions that may arise.

But this doesn't complete the employee benefits catalogue. A company can provide many other kinds of benefits—some that are especially important to a limited group of employees, some definitely in the "fringe" category. We shall now, in the final three sections, discuss a long list of these special benefits. However, the treatment of each will necessarily be much more brief.

For convenience, we have divided these benefits into three groups: "Special Services," such as child care and tuition refund programs, which, because of their nature, are used by only a limited number of employees—but can be especially important to those people; "Employment-Related Benefits," such as stock-purchase plans and relocation allowances, which have a direct link to the particular business circumstances of an individual company; and, finally, "Benefits Primarily for Executives."

CHILD CARE

Almost anyone gazing into a crystal ball to find out what the future holds for employee benefits will see child care looming large. The statistics alone point to some revolutionary changes: More than half of the mothers of children under six are now in the American work force. And, by 1990, there will be more than 10 million preschoolers with working mothers, to say nothing of an additional 20 million school-age children aged 5 to 13.

The numbers of two-earner families and single parents with young children continue to grow, which means that this is not just a passing phenomenon. It doesn't seem very likely that the day of the traditional family—with a nonworking mother at home to take care of the kids—will return in the foreseeable future...or ever.

So it's not at all surprising that talk about providing some sort of child-care assistance has been widespread in recent years. Not every executive agrees, of course. To many, taking care of children is a private affair—something toward which business should have a strictly hands-off policy. Perhaps so, but circumstances may dictate otherwise before long. If child-care assistance can reduce absenteeism, tardiness, and turnover (as statistics now seem to show it does); if the competition is providing child-care benefits; if the pool of new workers dries up to such an extent that only mothers of small children remain...then even the most hard-nosed executive may be forced to take a second look at the problem.

Child-care assistance is one benefit that many companies talk about but few actually have done anything about. Even though tax laws now give child care tax-deductible status, surprisingly few companies have yet taken advantage of this privilege. One reason, perhaps, is that they look at child care in an all-or-nothing fashion, perhaps feeling that the *only* option is to build their own day-care center where employees can drop off their children in the morning and pick them up after work.

This is one solution to the problem, of course—but one that very few companies have accomplished successfully. Actually, a number of alternatives are possible:

Information and referral services
This is the simplest and least expensive kind of child-care assistance, yet the one that the greatest number of parents may find useful—even those for whom child care is not a financial burden. It involves establishing some central point for gathering comprehensive lists of local child-care programs and providers: day-care centers, nursery schools, housekeepers, babysitters, and other facilities that employees may use.

The company doesn't match a particular employee with an appropriate child-care service; that remains the employee's responsibility. What the company *does* is provide as much information as possible about community facilities, profit-making and nonprofit child-care organizations, and available full-time and part-time workers with experience in taking care of children. Auxiliary services might include information about infant care, after-school activities for children, home care for sick children, and evening and weekend programs.

Setting up an information service of this kind requires a certain amount of effort and expense, of course, but once it's in operation the costs should be minimal. An alternative, particularly attractive to a smaller company, could be to use the services of an outside referral service, a number of which are now coming into existence.

Financial support
In this approach, the company's role is strictly dollars and cents. It doesn't get involved in any individual child-care programs; it simply agrees to share the cost by reimbursing employees for a portion of the costs of child care—either as cash repayment or by making some kind of discount arrangement with a child-care organization. This works most satisfactorily, of course, if the company has established some sort of flexible benefits program (see Chapter 4), where those who wish child-care cost reimbursement can choose it in lieu of some other benefit. In this way, any criticism that the company is unfairly providing a benefit to one group and not to another is avoided.

Flexible personnel policies
Among the ways in which a company's personnel policy can accommodate working mothers are:

- establishing a liberal allowance for maternity leave, either paid or unpaid;
- hiring mothers on a permanent part-time basis; and
- making job-sharing arrangements.

A policy of flexible working hours is another idea that has been well publicized in recent years. It involves setting up a sliding scale of working hours, so that some employees arrive early and leave early while others arrive late and leave late, with only a five- or six-hour core of time remaining at midday when the entire staff is on duty. (This arrangement, of course, is practical only for certain types of businesses.)

If this "flextime" can be worked out in a company, one of its obvious virtues is to make things a little easier for families in which both parents work; now they may be able to arrange their schedules so that at least one of them is home at the same time their children are.

Company day-care centers

The all-out approach—providing direct assistance to employees with preschool children by setting up an on-site day-care center—may be attractive if a company is interested in hiring large numbers of working mothers with young children. It also can be much easier to establish in some special cases where appropriate facilities are readily available—such as in a large metropolitan hospital. However, the idea has only been adopted by a very small number of companies, although a few large firms, notably Wang Laboratories and Corning Glass Works, are on the list.

What's involved here is the actual equipping and staffing of a full-fledged day-care nursery, either on company property or nearby. In this way, a company can closely monitor the quality of care that its employees' children are receiving, which will probably cost less than it would at an outside nursery.

Of course, a number of problems may present themselves. A company-sponsored day-care center usually is workable only where most employees live in the immediate vicinity. (A mother who must drive 20 miles from the suburbs into a central city may not be very enthusiastic about having her children commute along with her.)

Also, there are any number of licensing, zoning, insurance,

and staffing problems with which a company may not want to become involved. And, perhaps most important of all, a company may discover that its employees would really like to choose the kind of child care that best suits their own children—and that a company-run day-care center at their office or plant just isn't what they want.

SPECIAL CHILD CARE

Two special forms of child care that a few companies have recently begun to provide should also be mentioned here:

Adoption assistance

This is a benefit that will be greatly appreciated by a limited number of employees. It follows the logic that, since a company pays most of the costs of pregnancy and childbirth, why not do something for parents who choose to adopt a child? Adoption-assistance programs reimburse employees who legally adopt either an infant or older child, including such costs as adoption agency fees, legal expenses, pregnancy and hospital expenses of the natural mother, and immigration and naturalization expenses for a foreign-born child. Because of the very few times when this benefit will be used, a formal plan usually isn't necessary; employees can be paid all or a portion of their adoption expenses directly out of company funds.

Aid for handicapped children

Although a benefit of very limited application, this is one that is most welcome to those few families who need it. Parents of mentally retarded, emotionally disturbed, or physically handicapped children face heavy financial burdens, despite various federal and state programs designed to provide some assistance. A small number of companies have established formal programs to help defray the expenses of residential care, day care, special schools, or outpatient treatment for the handicapped children of their employees.

LEGAL SERVICES

Although group plans covering legal services have a long history, especially in Europe, they have never made much headway in this country until quite recently. General opposition from the legal profession and laws restricting the advertising of legal services have long held back the development of these arrangements.

But the need is there. The wealthy usually have their private attorneys and the very poorest can apply to Legal Aid, but the great middle class has no ready access to a lawyer. Yet, sooner or later, almost everyone ends up needing one—for a lawsuit, a divorce, transferring real estate, drawing up a will, or one of a host of other legal matters.

Labor unions have provided much of the impetus behind the introduction of legal services as a benefit (most noticeably, the United Auto Workers). And, in 1976, the tax laws were revised to make employer contributions to a prepaid legal-services plan tax deductible.

Although the spread of legal-services plans has not been as rapid as once was anticipated, many companies—especially those with flexible benefits programs—are looking at them as a possible new benefit to offer their employees. When in effect, they are used frequently and very much appreciated, and the cost is relatively low—usually in the neighborhood of $100 per employee per year.

Types of legal services plans

Two kinds are most common: the closed panel, in which a group of staff lawyers or participating attorneys handles all legal matters (working somewhat like a health maintenance organization); and the open panel, where the employee can use any lawyer, but is reimbursed only according to a prearranged schedule of fees—and is personally responsible for anything more than that amount. Some plans use a combination of closed and open panels.

To date, most legal-services plans have been sponsored by law firms and other organizations in the legal profession itself;

however, insurance companies are gradually getting into the act also.

What a plan covers
The basic service that every plan provides is consultation and legal advice—and often that's all that's needed. Most plans also include the drafting of wills and other relatively simple legal documents, bankruptcies, traffic offenses, and the transfer of real estate. Some group legal plans will also handle more complicated matters, such as domestic relations problems (divorce, legal separation, child custody, etc.); under other plans, these are excluded. Serious criminal matters, also, are covered only by a few of the most comprehensive legal plans.

Costs
A number of plans, especially those negotiated by the unions, are entirely company paid. Others may resemble medical insurance in their payment arrangements, with annual deductibles and copayment provisions.

PROPERTY AND LIABILITY INSURANCE

The idea seems logical enough: Companies provide employees with help in paying for their group health and life insurance—often footing the entire bill—so why not, as an extra benefit, give the same kind of help with other forms of insurance? After all, for most families today, their automobile insurance premium is the largest single insurance bill, and homeowner's insurance often is a close second.

However, this has been a very slow benefit to get off the ground, for some very good reasons. In the first place, under the law, an employer's contributions for these kinds of insurance are not tax deductible, as are those for group health and life, so such contributions would be considered taxable income for an employee. In addition, labor unions have shown no interest in this kind of insurance—in contrast to dental and legal services benefits—and thus have not blazed any trails that might lead to more general acceptance. Finally, many states have had laws forbidding group automobile insurance, under the reasoning that this would be discriminatory against drivers who were not members of a group. Most of these state laws now appear to be on the way out. But the prospects of *any* new benefit gaining tax-deductible status in the current governmental climate seem rather dim. (As we are seeing, it will be difficult enough to keep some long-established benefits tax deductible.)

Automobile insurance

One form of assistance that a limited number of employers have been providing is sponsorship of a *mass-merchandised* or *franchise* automobile-insurance plan. In many respects, this plan is no different from the insurance that an employee could obtain privately: Each person receives an individual policy and pays premiums based on the usual factors of age, sex, driving record, make of car, and so forth.

However, there are some definite advantages. Employees can pay for their insurance through regular payroll deductions, thus easing the impact of paying a large lump-sum premium once or twice a year. Also, premiums may actually be slightly less, because of smaller commissions. And employees, since they now represent a large customer, might hope to get better service when they file a claim. The only disadvantage could be the lack of flexibility; there's no choice of insurance companies.

Somewhere over the horizon lies *true group* automobile insurance. Here, one policy would cover all eligible employees in a company, who would each pay the same rate. This has all the advantages of the franchise plan, and, for high-risk people, it would mean lower premiums.

But a problem arises: To balance things out, low-risk drivers would be charged *more*, and, naturally, would be likely to pass up their company plan and look elsewhere for lower premiums, leaving the group plan with only the poor risks. In order to make the premium attractive to both high- and low-risk drivers, a true group plan usually must involve a fairly significant employer contribution. Although true group automobile insurance could be an interesting new employee benefit, it's another one that is unlikely to be accorded tax-deductible status.

Other property and liability insurance

Interest has been even more limited in plans that would make it possible for employees to pay their homeowner's, tenant's or personal-liability umbrella insurance through their companies. Such plans would encounter all the problems of group automobile insurance, and, since the differences in coverage vary so widely, would present even more complications. Also, a number of mortgage holders require that property insurance be paid in the same manner as mortgage payments, which would rule out any group arrangement.

TUITION REIMBURSEMENT

Tuition reimbursement occupies a peculiar position among employee-benefit plans. Although most larger firms have programs that refund part or all of the expense of job-related educational courses taken by employees, many of these plans have a very low profile. Often, only those employees who are genuinely interested will ever discover that their company actually does have a tuition-refund plan. In fact, some companies that have long had tuition-reimbursement plans are beginning to take a second look at the whole idea. Do these plans provide a genuine benefit or are they simply employee-relations gestures?

But this isn't the problem in a company with a large number of well-educated people, especially a high-technology firm where advanced degrees are commonplace. Here, a generous tuition-refund plan can be *the* benefit to stress in attracting ambitious young people; for them, tuition reimbursement can provide a way to begin a career and continue an expensive education at the same time.

One recent problem for tuition-refund plans has been their tax-deductible status, which has become something of a legislative football. Under a qualified plan, reimbursements to employees for approved educational courses are (when the law allows) deductible as a business expense by a company and not considered, as they once were, additional income for employees.

Questions to consider

Paying all or part of the cost of an educational program that an employee wants to take—especially one that will improve his or her job skills—might seem to be a fairly straightforward benefit. However, there are several important guidelines that must be agreed upon in setting up a tuition-reimbursement plan. Questions such as these must be answered:

- Should all tuition costs be paid, or only part? And, with partial payment, just what should be the percentage reimbursed? (50 percent once was fairly standard, but most programs pay more today.)
- Should books, registration charges, lab fees, and other incidental costs be included?
- What kind of courses should be eligible—those that are strictly job related or a much broader group?
- Can an employee pursue a college degree program including some required courses that, in themselves, are not job related?
- Who will be responsible for approving what an employee proposes to do?
- Should only courses at approved educational institutions be eligible? What about correspondence courses, adult education, business seminars, etc.?
- Should employees be reimbursed when they initially pay for the course, or after it is completed? In the latter case, should temporary tuition loans be available?

- What should be the limits on course loads and the total dollar amount of tuition?
- Will a student be required to achieve a certain minimum grade in a course?
- Should the program include paid time off when needed to take courses available only during working hours?

OTHER EDUCATIONAL ASSISTANCE

A company that is interested in supporting education need not limit itself to a standard tuition-reimbursement plan. Some other possibilities are:

Aid for employees' children
One good way to help educate the children of a company's employees is to give financial backing to a college scholarship program. A few firms have set up their own scholarships, but the most common procedure is to participate in the National Merit Scholarship program. Each year, outstanding high school students are selected through a series of competitive examinations, and these winners receive tuition awards based on family need. The National Merit Scholarship Corporation handles all the details of testing, selection, and payment; the participating company publicizes the program and agrees to pay awards to a fixed number of scholarship winners, or to all employees' children who become semifinalists or finalists.

Another way to help employees' children further their education is through a program of educational loans, handled either directly by the company or in cooperation with one of the federal or state student loan programs.

In-house courses
A number of companies have set up their own programs offering a range of educational courses. These may make use of the company's own resources, with classes being taught by

qualified company personnel or outside instructors, usually on company premises during lunchtime or after hours. Such topics as public speaking, speed reading, management techniques, business writing, computer use, and the like are often valuable to a wide range of employees. In firms where technical training is at a premium, the course list can be expanded in a number of appropriate directions.

More ambitiously, some companies, particularly those in disadvantaged urban areas, have recognized the need for in-house courses to train employees in remedial reading, elementary arithmetic, typing, shorthand, and other basic skills they have not acquired elsewhere.

PHILANTHROPY

Every company is inundated with appeals from the many charitable, cultural, and educational organizations that must rely to a great extent on contributions from business. Deciding on which of these worthy causes to support—and to what extent—can be a difficult chore. However, in making contributions to these organizations a company can, in somewhat indirect fashion, provide "benefits" that may be greatly appreciated by some of its employees.

Matching gifts
Many companies have set up formal programs under which they will match, dollar for dollar, a contribution that an employee makes to an educational or charitable institution. Certain guidelines are needed for a matching-gift program, such as limiting the gifts to certain categories of approved nonprofit organizations, putting minimum and maximum limits on the size of gifts that will be matched, and preparing the necessary forms and records. Like tuition reimbursement, matching-gift programs are employee benefits that often have been in existence at a company for a long time but, for some reason, have never received more than a minimum of publicity.

Free admissions
Another little-known auxiliary benefit can result from a company's charitable contributions. A cultural institution—museum, zoo, historical site, etc.—may agree to provide free or reduced-rate admissions to all employees of that company who identify themselves at the door.

EMPLOYMENT-RELATED BENEFITS

Although the benefits described in the following section may seem, at first glance, to be a miscellaneous assortment, they do have one common thread: Whether or not they are provided to employees by a company depends very much on that company's individual business situation—where it is located; its main business activity; and its own special history, customs, and traditions.

Recently, the Internal Revenue Service has turned its attention to a number of these employment-related benefits, especially subsidized eating facilities, personal trips in company planes, season tickets to sporting events, and discounts on company merchandise. In some cases, under regulations proposed late in 1985, these benefits are now considered as taxable income to employees. However, the IRS has also made clear that some other benefits of this kind—such as parking privileges, single tickets to sporting or theatrical events, occasional personal use of company office equipment and supplies, modest-priced holiday gifts, and company picnics—are specifically not taxable. (The IRS calls most of these "de minimis fringe benefits.")

GOVERNMENT-REQUIRED PROGRAMS

In addition to Social Security, which was described above, these include:

Unemployment compensation

In this country, unemployment compensation is the responsibility of a unique combination of federal and state agencies. A federal unemployment tax is assessed to each commercial or industrial employer, and each state also has its own separate tax. A company can offset its federal tax bill by up to 90 percent of the state unemployment tax it must pay. The federal government, in turn, gives grants to the states, and the states are responsible for running their own unemployment compensation systems—all of which have widely different standards of eligibility, waiting periods, number of weeks of payment, maximum and minimum payment, etc. During periods of severe unemployment, the federal government may add supplementary amounts to the unemployment compensation paid by the state systems.

In all the states, employer contributions are based on their individual experience rating, which depends on employee turnover. In three states (Alabama, Alaska, and New Jersey), small employee contributions to the unemployment compensation program are also required.

Workers' compensation

In a sense, workers' compensation is somewhat of an anachronism, since it dates back to the days of frequent industrial accidents and the lack of other disability insurance now available to injured workers.

Unlike unemployment compensation, this benefit is handled strictly on a state-by-state basis; there are no federal regulations, except those covering federal employees. Each state sets its own rules of eligibility for payments for job-related accidents or illnesses, as well as its own schedule of compensation, which may include temporary and permanent total disability pay, partial disability pay, medical reimbursement, rehabilitation, and survivor benefits. These all vary considerably from state to state.

In most states, employers may purchase workers' compensation insurance from an outside carrier, which will handle all claims and payments. Nineteen states operate their own workers' compensation insurance funds; in most of these states, an employer may use the state fund rather than an insurance company, but, in some, only the state insurance may be used. In almost all states, it's also possible for a company to self-insure against the risk of paying workers' compensation, possibly with reinsurance to cover the possibility of an extremely large claim.

Temporary disability benefits
In five states (California, Hawaii, New Jersey, New York, and Rhode Island) and in Puerto Rico, compulsory programs provide cash benefits to workers who are unable to work because of a nonoccupational disability. State funds have been established for these programs in all cases, but employers may also work through a private insurance company if they wish.

SUPPLEMENTAL UNEMPLOYMENT BENEFITS

Several of the larger labor unions, feeling that state unemployment benefits were not adequate, have negotiated supplemental unemployment benefit (SUB) plans with employers. These are most common in industries such as automobiles and steel, where much of the employment is cyclical. Under a SUB plan, employers either contribute a certain number of cents per employee-hour worked to a pooled fund, or set up individual accounts for their workers. Benefits are paid to laid-off employees that, when combined with state unemployment payments, can result in income that is very close to normal pay. However, there are no guarantees; benefits can be paid out only as long as there is money remaining in the SUB fund.

In addition to the financial support a SUB plan gives to the workers it covers, there's an additional benefit for employers: It may make their employees less prone to resist technological changes and more willing to accept necessary temporary layoffs.

RELOCATION ASSISTANCE

Asking an employee to pull up stakes in one city and move to another is never easy. When that employee has a family that has made more-or-less permanent ties in one community, the task is even harder. And it can be most difficult of all when, as is often the case these days, the employee has a spouse who is happily employed and not very enthusiastic about finding a new job in a new city.

In fact, more and more companies are finding out, sometimes to their chagrin, that employees will often refuse to undertake a relocation unless the new job represents a major career advancement. And, even then, some employees will turn down any job change that requires moving to a new city.

So, to soften the blow somewhat, companies have been liberalizing the monetary and other assistance they provide as reimbursement for the expenses of relocation. The easiest way to do this, of course, would simply be to pay out a flat dollar amount that seems sufficient to cover ordinary moving expenses, and let the employee take it from there.

But individual circumstances can be so radically different that this simple policy may not be fair to everyone—although it does avoid disagreements over exactly what is a justifiable moving expense. In any case, a more popular recourse is to set up a broad list of every conceivable expense that could be involved in a relocation from one city to another. The employee is reimbursed for whatever he or she must pay for any of these approved types of cost, which might include the costs involved in selling the employee's present home, in finding and purchasing a new one, and possibly for interim living expenses. And these expenses are no longer limited to homeowners, since companies are recognizing the fact that it costs renters to move these days, also.

Moving has become so common—and, at the same time so complicated—that a number of business services now specialize in employee relocation. The greatest assistance they can render is in the buying and selling of homes, where they often act as the middleman—purchasing a house from one transferred employee and reselling it to another.

In one sense, it probably could be argued that none of these reimbursements is actually a "benefit," since each simply repays an employee's legitimate expenses incurred in a move instigated by his employer. However, the Internal Revenue Service doesn't see it quite that way; it considers many of the items on a company's reimbursement schedule to be taxable income to the employee. So it has become a fairly widespread practice to "gross up" moving expense reimbursements to keep an employee from suffering a tax penalty.

Some special services to transferred employees may actually be more valuable than simply reimbursing moving expenses. A company can provide information so that a transferred employee can learn as much as possible about a new and probably unfamiliar part of the country—everything from maps of the region to personal introductions to new neighbors. Even more important can be assisting an employee's spouse in finding a satisfactory job in the new city. Often this can be the one most valuable service that a company can render—and the one that may finally persuade a reluctant employee to accept a transfer.

SUGGESTION PLANS

Formal systems designed to reward employees for making practical suggestions have a long history. But they must cast off the negative image of the old-time "suggestion box" seen (with its often unwelcome contents) in so many cartoons. For they are no laughing matter. In fact, of all the conceivable employee benefits, a suggestion system is the only one that is almost guaranteed to have a negative cost—yielding greater financial benefits to the company itself than to the employees who participate.

The National Association of Suggestion Systems estimates

that, for each dollar of administrative expense and cash awards that a company must outlay, a typical suggestion plan will return four dollars in cost savings, improved service, new products, or other improvements. And this, of course, does not include the intangible benefits: an enhanced feeling of genuine participation in a company's business efforts, greater job satisfaction, improved two-way communication between employees and management, or recognition of the work of previously unheralded lower-level workers.

However, despite all this, many companies' suggestion plans have failed through lack of attention by management. If employees find that their suggestions are rejected out of hand or (perhaps worse) not answered, they will cease submitting them and the plan will die.

To succeed, a suggestion system must observe a number of guidelines, including:

- The system must be supported by management, given constant publicity, and, if necessary, supplied with full-time personnel to keep it running efficiently.
- Rules must be established to define what kinds of suggestions are eligible and what are not (such as, for example, new advertising slogans or employee benefits).
- Exactly who can participate must be made clear; managers, for example, usually should not be rewarded for ideas concerning their regular areas of responsibility.
- A fair procedure must be set up to handle the submission of an idea—with the proper forms and clear, simple instructions.
- It must be decided whether a suggester's anonymity is to be preserved. (Once the standard practice was for ideas to be submitted in secret; now, suggesters are often encouraged to discuss their ideas with their supervisors.)
- Suggestions must be promptly acknowledged and judged fairly, and final decisions must be reported rapidly (even if it's not yet possible to put a new idea into effect). And the reasons for rejecting an idea should be explained honestly

and tactfully. (Don't imply: "We thought of that years ago, you dummy.")
- An award system must be established that includes a reasonably generous minimum reward for any acceptable suggestion (some companies use merchandise rather than cash), a mechanism for rewarding ideas that result in specific financial benefits to the company (such as a percentage of the estimated cost savings during one year), and a means of giving fair rewards to intangible ideas or ones for which it is impossible to measure dollar benefits accurately.

COMMUTATION ASSISTANCE

Today, very few people live over the store or can walk down the street to their jobs. Simply getting to work can be a major burden for many employees. Traveling long distances from home, fighting traffic, finding parking space, or putting up with decaying public transportation can bring people to their jobs in a low state of morale before they even begin work.

Thus it is somewhat surprising how little attention these problems receive from many companies; the feeling often seems to be that how employees get to work and get back home is strictly their own business. Companies that have established plants and offices in rural or suburban areas, of course, are much more cognizant of the need for adequate parking space and access roads. But long-established businesses in central cities, not even needing to provide a company parking lot, are much more likely to ignore commutation assistance as a legitimate employee benefit.

One practice now possible under the tax laws is for companies to purchase transit passes from the local transportation authority and resell them to employees at a discount. Although this idea has met with mixed success in the limited number of cities where it has been tried, it may have a brighter future as improvements in urban transportation continue and the use of electronically controlled weekly or monthly passes becomes more widespread.

One means of aiding commutation that has been specifically singled out by the IRS is van pooling. Under present tax laws, a company may provide vans for transporting employees to and from work, with the cost being considered a tax-free benefit.

Other ways to ease the burden of employee commutation might include:

- the encouragement of employee car pooling through a centralized information system (an idea that always seems to crop up at times of energy crisis and die down once gasoline prices decline);
- subsidizing parking in public lots when the company cannot provide adequate parking facilities; and
- promoting and supporting new bus routes that could be used by large numbers of employees.

CREDIT UNIONS

This is a long-established benefit whose value to the ordinary employee can often be underestimated by an executive with easy access to other financial resources. Credit unions offer employees a convenient way to save through payroll deductions (especially if their company doesn't have its own thrift or savings plan), as well as a means of obtaining low-cost personal loans. In recent years, many states have eased their rules on credit unions, and, as a result, some of them have begun to provide checking accounts, charge cards, money-market accounts, and similar banking services.

A credit union is one benefit that, under the law, a company itself cannot set up and run. It must be controlled by employees, who elect their own officers and establish policies under guidelines set by the Bureau of Federal Credit Unions or the various state organizations.

But if its employees do form a credit union, a company can provide such support as office space, publicity in internal communications, and access to the payroll deduction system. The minor cost of this assistance is usually very worthwhile to a company, since a credit union can reduce the need for employees to ask for emergency financial help or special pay advances.

STOCK PURCHASE PLANS

Earlier, we discussed stock-ownership plans, under which employees can acquire shares of their company's common stock at no cost under a bonus or profit-sharing arrangement. Many firms whose stock is publicly held also offer their employees the chance to buy shares with their own money.

In most cases, employees can sign up for a regular investment through payroll deductions. This offers both convenience and the opportunity for "dollar cost averaging," since the fixed dollar amount that is deducted will purchase a different number of shares each time—more when the price is low, fewer when it is high.

Other advantages are reduced commission costs—or none at all—plus the tendency to leave one's investment in company shares untouched, with dividends to be reinvested in additional shares of stock.

This is a simple enough benefit—yet, every now and then, you hear of a long-time employee of a successful company who has invested a modest amount in the firm's stock over the years, and is now about to retire with a block of shares worth hundreds of thousands of dollars.

MERCHANDISE DISCOUNTS

Giving employees an opportunity to buy their company's products or services at a discount offers them some cash savings and encourages the use of the company's own merchandise. The practice is most common among consumer-goods companies, and some have even set up stores on their premises to sell items at cost or substantially reduced prices. Some even give them away.

This benefit is also popular in a number of service businesses; the airlines, in particular, have long used the possibility of free or greatly discounted travel for employees and their families as a recruiting inducement. It's also common for educational institutions to offer free or reduced tuition to the children of faculty and other staff members, for banks to give free checking accounts to their employees, and so forth.

With some imagination, many other companies could probably do likewise. It costs very little, but the yield in improved employee relations can be attractive. Recent tax rulings made it clear that most purchase discounts of this kind—especially those that a company provides "at no additional cost to itself"—are not considered taxable income to an employee.

GIFTS

Very few companies still hand out Christmas turkeys, but awarding outright cash gifts or bonuses on a regular basis is still fairly common in some industries. It's seen most often in smaller firms, especially in the financial community, where year-to-year earnings are unpredictable and subject to severe ups and downs. In good years, the bonus will be very generous; in bad years, it may be nonexistent.

Most companies that give these bonuses base the annual allotment on a percentage of salary, with length of service and job level often being an added consideration. All such money, of course, is considered part of an employee's ordinary taxable earnings.

Like some other benefits, such as cash distributions from profit sharing, a gift that is awarded regularly comes to be anticipated as a matter of course—and thus loses any special impact, except when it is unusually large. But the negative effects of a less-than-expected gift can be much worse. For these and other reasons, many companies that traditionally had been awarding cash gifts are now beginning to take a look at other alternatives, such as thrift/savings plans or Section 401[k] arrangements.

SUBSIDIZED FOOD SERVICE

Not too long ago, it was fairly common practice for employers with many low-level clerical employees, such as the large insurance companies, to offer a free lunch as a benefit. From the companies' point of view, this had two positive aspects: It diverted some attention from the relatively low salaries they were paying, and it kept employees' lunchtime to a minimum, since shifts could be marched in and out of the company cafeteria at 25- or 30-minute intervals.

Now, except in very isolated instances, or where employees are on duty during mealtime (such as restaurant employees or airline crew members on a flight), there's no more free lunch. However, many companies feel that providing food service whose cost is subsidized, at least in part, is a necessity. This is particularly true, of course, for companies in rural or suburban locations, where there's simply nowhere else to go for lunch. Even in the central city, a company may feel that providing attractive low-cost meals will, among other things, reduce the need for employees to take extended time off for lunch.

In the past, running the cafeteria or dining room was a company's own responsibility; now it's more common (and certainly much less of a headache) to turn the entire operation over to an outside concessionaire, who prepares and serves meals on premises supplied by the company.

HEALTH AND RECREATION PROGRAMS

Although companies have for a long time sponsored softball teams, bowling leagues, and other organized athletic activities, the current emphasis on maintaining health and physical fitness has given extra impetus to this kind of employer involvement (see "'Wellness' Programs" earlier in this chapter). Many firms have begun to see value in setting up gyms, running tracks, or other athletic facilities on their own property if space is available, or in subsidizing memberships in local health clubs.

Nor does it require setting up a complete internal medical department for a company to participate in important health screening programs, such as those for high blood pressure, diabetes, and early cancer detection, or to encourage its employees to participate in training courses in cardiopulmonary resuscitation, first aid, and the like.

EMPLOYEE CLUBS AND ACTIVITIES

Depending on a company's individual climate and traditional "culture," it may or may not be heavily involved in organizing and running an extensive program of employee clubs and other recreational activities. The largest employer in a small town with few leisure-time possibilities will be much more likely to do so than will a company based in a large city, where most employees may want to head home as soon as the working day ends.

Employees of some large companies can select from an impressive assortment of clubs, discount tickets, travel opportunities, and the like, sometimes even with company personnel assigned to full-time duty coordinating the activities.

SERVICE AWARDS

Finally, we come to an employee benefit that, although one of the most traditional, may be one about which employees have mixed feelings. To younger people in particular, the very idea of honoring long-time employees with some kind of symbolic award may smack of old-time paternalism. But, to someone who has put in a quarter century of loyal service to a company without any recognition except a regular paycheck and a few modest promotions, a 25-year pin or being invited to a Quarter Century Club dinner may be much more important than might be imagined. Service awards, especially, represent the kind of benefit whose importance depends almost entirely on each individual company's own traditional patterns of behavior.

BENEFITS PRIMARILY FOR EXECUTIVES

The care and feeding of top executives, while a most important concern for almost any company, is somewhat outside the scope of this book. Vast amounts of material on the subject of executive compensation are available, to say nothing of the many consulting firms for whom this is a primary area of expertise.

However, we shall close this discussion of the complete array of employee benefits that are provided by businesses by mentioning some of the things that are often provided to those at the top of their companies. We do this for one reason: The dividing line between what is strictly an executive benefit—or "perk" if you will—and what is offered to the broad range of employees is becoming less and less distinct. Especially with the onset of flexible benefits programs, companies are finding it makes sense to offer as a special option to all employees some less-familiar benefits that, heretofore, had been available only to its top echelon.

SPECIAL COMPENSATION ARRANGEMENTS

We must mention at the first a form of benefit that, by its very nature, will definitely not be offered to a broad range of employees—individualized compensation arrangements, such as *performance bonuses*, which directly tie a significant amount of an executive's compensation to achieving certain agreed-upon company or individual goals, and *deferred-compensation* arrangements, in which a certain portion of an executive's annual compensation is not paid immediately (and thus is not taxable) but is deferred until some later time, such as when he or she reaches retirement age.

In many cases, the details of these special compensation arrangements are set up on an individual basis, often being included under special contractual agreements with the executives concerned. And, of course, sometimes an extraordinary form of compensation may be arranged with the express purpose of hiring a particularly outstanding individual away from another firm.

SUPPLEMENTAL RETIREMENT PLANS

Another benefit that, by definition, is restricted to the top levels of management is the supplemental executive retirement plan, or SERP. This is a form of deferred compensation that offers extra benefits when a high-level executive retires. In essence, a SERP is a nonqualified plan that has been especially designed to provide retirement income above the maximum amounts allowed for pension plans in general.

A company may have a number of reasons for setting up such a plan for its executives:

- The objective of a company's pension plan may be to provide a certain percentage of replacement income to all employees after retirement; because of the legal maxi-

mums on pension payments, the regular plan may not provide this percentage to highly paid executives.
- A supplemental plan can give pension credit for executive bonuses or deferred compensation, which would not be covered under the rules of the general pension plan.
- It can be used as a recruiting tool, to guarantee that an executive hired in mid- or late career will not suffer because of limited years of coverage under a company's regular plan.
- It can be used to encourage executives to take early retirement without losing pension income (the "open window").
- Or, on the other hand, it can be a means of keeping an executive with a company, at least to early retirement age ("golden handcuffs").

As long as a SERP pays unfunded benefits only to a limited number of "highly compensated" executives, it must meet only a few legal requirements; usually a plan can be specially tailored to fit the needs of each company and its executives. (However, there are many legal restrictions on "top-heavy" provisions in qualified retirement plans.)

STOCK OPTIONS

Once strictly the province of the top executives, many companies in recent years have begun to offer stock options to a fairly broad echelon of middle management. They come in two varieties: (1) options that are worth something only if the company's stock increases significantly in price ("appreciation-only" plans) and (2) those whose value is not dependent on an increase in stock price ("full-value" plans).

The first group includes:

- *Nonqualified stock options*, which simply give someone a right to purchase a specified number of shares at any time within a certain period (such as 10 years) at the stock's

present price; the difference between the fair market price when the option is cashed in and this original price is taxable income.
- *Stock appreciation rights (SARs)*, which avoid the problem of raising cash to purchase stock under a nonqualified plan (a particular problem for corporate "insiders" who may be restricted from immediately selling some of their newly acquired shares to do this). With an SAR, the executive receives only the difference between the fair market price and the option price—usually in the form of cash, although this amount may also be translated into an equivalent value in shares of stock.
- *Incentive stock options (ISOs)*, which are becoming increasingly popular, since they are subject to a number of special tax rules that make it possible to purchase shares without being immediately liable to income tax; shares held for one year become subject only to long-term capital gains taxes.

Full-value stock plans can involve:

- *performance shares*, which are shares of stock awarded according to a prearranged formula that is related to the achievement of certain company or individual performance goals;
- *performance units*, which are very similar, but based on some figure other than stock price, such as a multiple of earnings;
- *restricted stock*, or shares that are awarded to an executive but may not be sold or pledged until a certain period has passed; leaving the company before then means that the stock is forfeited;
- *dividend units*, which are equivalent to shares of company stock with awards being paid out whenever dividends are paid to stockholders; and
- *phantom stock*, in which no actual stock is issued, but the executive receives payments equal to any increase in market value (plus the dividends paid out) on a certain number of shares.

FINANCIAL COUNSELING

This is one of the fastest-growing executive benefits, and one that seems likely to be extended downwards to a broader group of employees. It has become quite common for companies to offer a number of their top executives the services of a specialist in financial planning—sometimes a company employee, more often a representative of one of the growing number of independent financial-counseling organizations. The reasoning is that providing this service will relieve executives of the time and worry of doing this kind of planning on their own.

Financial counseling may include extensive analysis of an executive's assets, estate planning, preparation of a will and annual tax returns, advice on the proper use of the company's benefit-plan opportunities, information about tax-shelter possibilities, investment management, and similar concerns.

Of course, some negatives must be considered. First, individualized financial planning of this kind is relatively expensive; it may cost as much at $3,000—or more—per executive to start, plus continuing annual fees of $1,000 or $2,000. Also, some executives may feel that they are perfectly able to handle their own finances without the interference of an outside service selected by their company. And there's the possible (but remote) danger that the company could be held legally responsible for bad advice given to one of its executives.

All financial counseling, however, need not be of this Rolls-Royce variety. There are also mass-marketed financial planning services, usually involving group meetings and seminars, together with a certain amount of individual financial analysis and advice, that are priced in the $100-an-employee range. As everyone's finances seem to get more complicated, this kind of counseling may become a more widely offered employee benefit.

The tax treatment of financial counseling is somewhat unusual. Whatever a company spends is considered part of an executive's compensation, and this amount must be included as taxable income. However, this penalty is balanced by the fact that the same amount can be listed as a deductible ("miscellaneous") expense in the executive's itemized tax return.

EXECUTIVE PERQUISITES

Not long ago—when taxes at the highest salary levels were much greater and government agencies less strict—companies had strong incentives to provide executives with various kinds of noncash compensation in the form of special perquisites. Today, however, most companies insist that the perks they offer be both tax effective and justifiable as legitimate business expenses. The lavish company yacht and the overseas junket combining one day of work with seven of pleasure travel have become things of the past.

Executive perks today are designed not just to increase the size of a compensation package; they also can *individualize* an executive's compensation. Thus, in designing them, a company is wise to consider the personal needs and interests of individual executives—not just decide on some nice new perk and offer it across the board. (A company car, after all, isn't too exciting to an executive who happens to live in a city apartment three blocks from his office.)

One negative aspect to all special executive benefits and privileges cannot be ignored, however. A number of companies, perhaps influenced by the apparent success of more egalitarian Japanese-style management, have begun to question whether the value gained from special treatment for executives may not be outweighed by the resentment these perks may produce in the general employee population.

Here are some of the more commonly offered executive perquisites that haven't yet been mentioned:

"In-house" perks. Individually decorated offices, multiple windows, executive dining rooms, special electronic or telecommunications equipment, and reserved parking space are all standard badges of office.

Extended benefits. Many companies offer extra vacation time or extended group life and long-term disability insurance beyond that included in the standard policy; special medical expense reimbursement may cover 100 percent of family bills (an increasingly costly benefit today).

Clubs. Memberships in luncheon clubs that are regularly used for business meetings are common; country clubs seem to raise a red flag to the IRS and are much more difficult to claim as a necessary business expense.

Company cars. A chauffeur-driven vehicle for the CEO can usually be justified for security reasons, particularly by a large, visible corporation. Tax laws, however, are now cracking down on "luxury" cars for executives, and personal use of any business vehicle is receiving greater scrutiny from the IRS. (Company airplanes are getting even more attention.)

Expense accounts. At one time, a top executive could expect to receive a fairly lavish sum on top of salary for "expenses"—with no detailed accounting being required as to exactly where this money went. But this practice, like some of the other traditional perks, has caught the attention of the IRS and is passing into limbo.

Living quarters. The use of a company apartment, unless it can be justified as a business expense, is considered taxable compensation; this has also become a much less common perk.

Interest-free or low-interest loans. Some executives may value these for unexpected housing or education expenses; the only taxable feature might be "imputed" interest.

Executive physical examinations. These are one of the most widely offered perquisites.

Special air travel. First-class air accommodations were once standard practice for executives; now some companies with cost-cutting programs may make them use "business class" or discount rates whenever possible—or even sit in the back of the plane. Another possible cloud on the horizon: a proposal to consider bonus travel under "frequent flyer" programs as taxable income.

3
FLEXIBLE BENEFITS

It's now time to discuss in detail an important and fast-growing concept in employee benefits management: flexible benefits. It is so new an idea that even its name has not yet become standardized. What we call "flexible benefits" can also go under such labels as "flexible compensation," "optional benefits," "variable benefits," and so forth.

The term "cafeteria plan" has also come into widespread use—particularly in governmental circles. This name is colorful enough, but it carries the unwelcome (and misleading) connotation that a flexible benefits program, somehow, offers employees a tempting array of goodies that aren't available to most other working people. But, as we shall see, this is not at all the case. Nevertheless, *cafeteria plan* is the official term used in Section 125 of the Internal Revenue Code, which describes the specific kinds of choices between taxable and nontaxable benefits that the federal government recognizes.

Whatever its name, a flexible benefits program has one essential element: It offers an *individual* combination of benefits to each employee, rather than a standard program that covers all employees in the same way.

WHY HAVE A FLEXIBLE BENEFITS PROGRAM?

The basic reasoning behind flexible benefits is really very simple: Why should a company provide the identical benefits for each employee? Why not make allowances for the vast differences in their needs and family circumstances? Why spend money for benefits that people don't have any use for?

No matter how hard it tries, a company cannot devise a benefits program that is ideal for each of its employees; the range in individual situations is too wide. One employee will want the best possible life insurance coverage; another will be almost totally uninterested in it. One employee will want the fullest possible family medical protection; another employee may already be included as a dependent under his or her spouse's plan.

As with so many other aspects of employee benefits today, it is the changing face of the American working population that, more than anything else, makes it virtually impossible for any benefits program to be best for everyone. More and more, a company will find itself with people on the payroll who don't fit the conventional mold: two income families, single parents, and mature women returning to the labor force. The typical benefits program, in most cases, won't do a very good job for any of them.

Another driving force behind the move to flexibility, of course, has been the spectacular rise in cost for almost all kinds of benefits, especially medical plans. As employee benefits come to represent a larger and larger percentage of total payroll expenses, companies have, not surprisingly, become much more concerned about getting their money's worth from what they are spending. And thus the cost of providing benefits that a substantial number of employees neither need nor want becomes especially high.

A few words of caution are in order here, however. When the concept of flexible benefits first gained attention, there was considerable talk that it would be a wonderful way for a company to save a lot of money on benefits. Flexible benefits have many admirable features, but truly impressive savings on total benefit expenses is not high on the list—at least not in the short run. However, almost any company that adopts a well-planned flexible program will find that each dollar it spends on employee benefits is being put to better use.

Finally, another important trend must be recognized. The working population today—particularly its younger members—won't simply accept without question what a company provides. More and more, employees want to have a voice in deciding what benefits they receive; if a company doesn't listen to this voice, it can be heard in other ways—such as with the adi of a labor union. A flexible program, if nothing else, gives each employee an opportunity to make some important personal decisions about his or her own benefits. And it can give employees a chance—often for the first time—to understand the real cost of their benefits.

THE ORIGINS OF FLEXIBLE BENEFITS

At its heart, the idea of flexible benefits is not at all revolutionary. Any benefit plan that has an optional feature—such as whether to include dependents under a medical plan—is, in the strictest sense, a flexible benefit. And many long-established company benefits programs include a definitely "flexible" element if they allow an employee the option to sign up for extra life insurance, a dental plan, or something else that is financed partially or totally by his or her own contributions.

Today's full-fledged flexible benefits programs go far beyond these rudimentary options, however. They allow employees to make some significant choices between various plans—or even to forego them entirely and substitute something else, such as additional vacation time or cash.

The kinds of plans we are discussing did not make their

appearance until the 1970s, when three well-publicized forerunners of today's flexible programs were introduced by American Can Company, Educational Testing Service, and TRW. For several years, these three remained lonely outposts, with the rest of the benefits world observing their fate. Each of them introduced flexibility in a different way, but all proved to be very successful—in both achieving their goals and avoiding the predicted pitfalls. (In the section, Flexible Benefits Programs—Some Examples, below, we'll describe these three companies' plans as they exist today—incorporating all the changes and improvements that experience has recommended.)

The federal government recognized flexible benefits in 1978, when Section 125 was added to the Internal Revenue Code. Then, in the mid-1980s, the period of observation concluded, and the overall movement toward flexible benefits commenced. As many companies have adopted the concept, it has assumed an impressive variety of forms, offering a wide range of flexibility. Some recent plans offer only a limited number of choices, and are "flexible" in name only; others go well beyond the degree of flexibility provided in any of the original programs. The trend has been helped along, of course, by a multitude of benefits consultants, who have been eager to assist any company whose thoughts turn toward flexible benefits.

A parallel development has been the growing popularity of various kinds of *flexible spending accounts*. These are somewhat different from the broad-based flexible benefits programs we are describing here—although a flexible program may include a flexible spending account as one of its components.

The course has not been completely smooth, however; some companies have discovered that switching to flexible benefits is, in practice, more complicated than anticipated—and have been disappointed in the results.

Nevertheless, the arguments in favor of flexible benefits appear to be so substantial that the movement toward giving employees more of a choice in arranging their own benefits packages seems inevitable.

SOME BASIC PRINCIPLES

Making the decision to adopt a flexible benefits program—and all the costs and preparatory work that are involved—is not something to be undertaken lightly. Before doing so, a company might ponder the following:

If it ain't broke, don't fix it
This would seem obvious, but it's a truism that has been ignored by some companies. If your benefits program is perfectly satisfactory—employees like it and haven't complained and costs are not out of line—why change it? All too frequently a benefits manager (or CEO), carried along by the wave of publicity, will suggest a radical, but unnecessary, overhauling of a company's program. As we shall try to explain in this section, flexible benefits have many things going in their favor, but they are not necessarily the best solution for everyone. And, since switching to flexible benefits is not easy—and may actually increase costs, especially at the beginning—no company should do so without carefully analyzing its own special situation.

Know your people
Every company's mix of employees is unique. And, since the rationale for flexible benefits is to make a better match between employee needs and benefit plans, it's obviously very important to know these employees well. The most successful flexible benefits plans have been those that emerged from sound research into exactly who made up a company's staff and what their specific needs were.

Finding this out isn't easy. It shouldn't be done by guesswork or by seat-of-the-pants logic. Employee attitudes toward benefits are often quite different from what "expert" opinion has said they were. In most companies, employees have little opportunity to discuss, criticize, or question their benefits package. And, when they finally do get the opportunity to speak up, what they have to say may be quite surprising. The retirement plan that management has always thought was wonderful may be viewed with skepticism; the medical plan may be bogged down with annoying red tape; the lack of a dental plan may be strongly resented. And some employees may be thoroughly disenchanted with benefits in general.

As we shall discuss in Chapter 5, surveying employee attitudes is never a job for amateurs. And, in studying flexible benefits—where decisions may involve substantial sums of money—it's extremely important that these decisions be based on the most accurate knowledge about the employees who will be affected by them.

Set realistic goals

Employees may have strong feelings about their benefits, but they aren't paying all the bills. Left on their own, employees would probably like to have much more than management is willing to provide—or can afford. Benefits such as a prescription drug plan, group automobile insurance, or an on-site daycare center might be very popular with some employees—but not necessarily ones that the company would want to sponsor. So the goals for a new flexible benefits program, as for any benefit plan, should be a fair compromise between a company's objectives and its employees' wish lists.

Decide upon some basic benefits

It's unrealistic to leave all the decisions up to the employee. As just mentioned, a company may feel that certain essential benefits must be provided—even if some employees think they don't need them. A flexible benefits plan, therefore, is rarely *completely* flexible. A few "core" benefits are virtually always provided, in one way or another, to every employee. This basic group of benefits will vary from company to company, depending on each organization's individual benefits philosophy. In most cases, however, it will include some paid vacation, a medical plan of some kind, a retirement-income program, and a minimum amount of life insurance. None of these is sacred; the argument could be made that, for some employees, even the most "basic" benefit is unnecessary.

Sometimes, however, a company may feel obligated to provide a relatively unpopular benefit. For example, employees may have little interest in long-term disability insurance, believing that this is something they'll never need. But management may recognize the potential long-term costs of having just one employee permanently incapacitated—and the resulting negative publicity if this employee were completely uninsured, even by personal choice. So the company might well decide that long-term disability insurance is something that is too important to be optional.

On the other hand, there is a real danger in making the core too large. If the optional elements in the plan are too few or the real choices too limited, the plan may become "flexible" in name only, and hardly worth the trouble to introduce.

All of this means, therefore, that deciding exactly what benefits to include in the core—and how much of each to provide—is one of the toughest decisions to be made in designing a flexible benefits program.

Build upon the basics

It's after the basic, universal benefits have been decided on and put in place that the real flexibility begins. Under one popular system, the plan provides each employee with a certain amount of credits to be allocated among an assortment of benefits according to his or her individual preference. The credits may be the same for every employee or, more often, be based on years of service, salary, job level, or a combination of these.

In fact, many companies are finding that this formula for flexible-credit allocation offers a chance to relate benefits to salary—and, to a lesser extent, length of service—in a way that isn't possible in conventional programs. One flexible plan, for example, gives everyone $900 worth of annual benefits credits, plus an additional amount equal to 1 percent of salary and a flat $10 for each year of service. Under this formula, therefore, a 20-year employee making $40,000 a year would receive $1,500 in annual benefits credits ($900 + $400 + $200), while a five-year employee earning $20,000 would get $1,150 ($900 + $200 + $50).

In any case, an employee knows exactly how many credits he or she has to allocate to the available optional benefits, together with the "cost" of each option—either in actual dollars or some other kind of measurement such as "flexible credits." (Usually this information is printed right on the employee's annual enrollment form.)

The employee then selects benefits in any combination, with the only restriction being that the costs for the various selections must add up to the designated total. In some plans, a number of these credits may be allocated to a special *flexible spending account*, which can later be used for medical costs not paid by the regular plan, (such as a deductible) or for child care or legal expenses. (As explained later in this chapter, the IRS has issued special rules for flexible spending accounts, which may only be used to pay for these three kinds of benefits.)

The options usually don't end there, either. In most plans, employees have the opportunity to select additional benefits beyond those that are covered by their allotment of company-provided credits. These extras can be paid for through after-tax payroll deductions, with pretax or "salary reduction" payments, or by means of a flexible spending account.

Don't make choices too difficult

Selecting your own benefits is always hard, particularly the first time it must be done. Some important decisions are involved—decisions that most employees have never had to make. This means that a plan should provide a fairly limited number of choices, with the differences among the alternatives being easy to recognize. (It's unrealistic to expect *anyone* to decide sensibly among eight different medical plans or a dozen kinds of investments.)

One way of reducing the complications is to offer employees alternative groups of benefits, or "modules," rather than forcing them to go through the whole program, benefit by benefit, as they make their choices.

Make allowances for future changes
It's asking a lot of most employees to have them make final choices about their own benefits programs. This is especially true at the beginning, when the whole idea of flexible benefits may be entirely new. In all likelihood, some employees, sooner or later, will have second thoughts—and realize that they've made a mistake in their choices. So it's important to set up a convenient way for employees to amend those choices.

More changes will come later on, too. One of the great advantages of a flexible benefits program, after all, is that it is specifically designed to take care of employees' evolving needs.

Pay attention to details
A flexible benefits program, whatever its form, will inevitably result in greater administrative responsibilities for a company's benefits department. Poor administration, probably more than anything else, can damage a new flexible benefits program badly. It's important to make sure that all the details of a new program are in place before it's even announced to employees. Simple, easy-to-fill-out forms and clearly worded instructions are essential. Employees' choices must be honored quickly and accurately; payroll deductions, if required, must be made in the correct amounts.

Establishing an entirely new kind of benefits arrangement is not a job for amateurs—especially with the tax-law complications that may loom ahead. And, if no one in a company's organization has the experience—or time—to handle this challenging job, outside consultants will be more than happy to lend a hand.

Remember that good communication is all-critical
As we shall explain in Chapter 6, communication is an essential aspect of any benefits program—but one that, unfortunately, often receives much less attention than it deserves. And, with a new idea like flexible benefits, it's particularly important that employees receive complete, accurate information in clear, understandable language.

THE ARGUMENTS AGAINST FLEXIBLE BENEFITS

Before going any further, we might stop and consider this: If a flexible benefits program has so much going for it, why isn't the idea more popular? When the concept was first put into practice—back in the 1970s—only a handful of firms were involved, and progress was painfully slow for a number of years. Recently, many more companies have switched to completely flexible benefits programs; others have taken partial strides in that direction, such as introducing the free-standing flexible spending accounts or adding flexible options to long-established benefit plans.

However, despite all this activity, these companies still represent a small fraction of American business. For the great majority, flexible benefits remains uncharted territory. And this certainly isn't because of any general lack of interest in new ideas on the part of the benefits community. For, as we have seen with the rapid and widespread adoption of Section 401[k] plans, there seem to be no inhibitions against new benefits that offer immediate financial incentives.

The arguments in favor of the flexible benefits concept, on the other hand, require a longer period of time to prove themselves. And, over the short run, a number of legitimate questions can be raised—any of which might persuade a company to continue taking a wait-and-see attitude toward flexible benefits. Here are some of them:

"Administration is impossible"

A few years ago this would have been much more persuasive. But, even if it's less true today, it's a legitimate criticism. No one can ignore the fact that administering a flexible benefits program, especially at the very beginning, is a challenging task.

In those difficult days just before a new program is announced, the administrative detail connected with a flexible benefits program may seem much greater than with a more conventional arrangement. However, once a flexible program is in place, it can be administered on a day-to-day basis almost as easily as a conventional benefits program—thanks, in large part, to the wonders of modern electronic data processing.

"It would be impossible to explain"

Certainly, good communication is vital. And the skeptics have been proved wrong here also, since there's now a growing list of communications success stories. Any company that commits itself to taking the time and trouble to inform its employees about flexible benefits has many examples to follow—and consultants to provide the assistance, if need be.

Success, of course, builds upon success. As time goes by, the concept of flexibility is becoming much more widely recognized and, to some extent, understood by the general public—even if it goes under the unfortunate label of "cafeteria plan." The job of communicating the basic idea of flexible benefits, therefore, is becoming much easier.

"Flexible benefits won't save us any money"

Unfortunately, that may be true, but that usually isn't the best reason to switch to flexible benefits in the first place. One of the early arguments in favor of a flexible plan was that it would be an excellent way to contain rising medical costs. And some companies *have* succeeded in putting a dent in their health-insurance costs. But this hasn't happened as often as had been hoped. Most flexible programs have been plagued by the same upward price movements that have affected everyone else.

Of course, given the opportunity to choose among a number of medical plans, some employees have selected the least expensive coverage. But these people have often been counterbalanced by others who, whether they really need it or not, will always opt for the highest possible level of coverage.

"Adverse selection will ruin all our calculations"

According to insurance company theory, the people who need a benefit the most will sign up for it in the greatest numbers—and thus the carefully calculated premium rates (based on the population as a whole) will turn out to be too low. But this "adverse selection" has also proved to be much less serious than professional Cassandras had feared.

To some extent, adverse selection will always occur. People with bad teeth *are* more likely to spend their optional dollars on dental insurance. But real human beings don't always act in the carefully programmed way that insurance company computers predict they will. Some employees who are in the best of health and have no great family responsibilities will still, for their own reasons, sign up for the maximum level of life insurance. And others will do just the opposite.

Of course, the lurking danger of adverse selection is always present when relatively few cases are involved, and this might well prevent a smaller company from self-funding a flexible benefits program.

"Employees will make unwise decisions about benefits"

The old paternalistic argument that "we know what's best for our employees" still has support in some quarters. And, occasionally, employees *do* give validity to this idea. They'll pass up needed benefits in favor of a maximum amount of vacation time or cash. Or they'll allocate their benefits dollars to plans they really have no use for.

That will always happen. Some people simply don't have the maturity or experience to make the best choices for themselves. But should everyone else suffer as a result? To the surprise of many skeptics, employees in the established flexible benefits plans have, for the most part, made reasonably intelligent and conservative choices.

And it isn't simply a question of paternalism. Try as it may, no company can know the full details of each employee's family situation—the things that will determine, in the long run, how he or she chooses among a variety of potential benefit plans. The young single woman may be the sole support of aged parents in a nursing home. The married man with two small children may have a working wife who is highly paid executive. These days, you never can tell. And it's an arrogant—and foolhardy—company that thinks it can, in its wisdom, design a benefits program that will automatically be best for everyone.

To Sum Up

Experience has shown that many of the anticipated problems with flexible benefits have, in reality, turned out to be much less severe than had been feared. Companies with well-designed programs—and ones that have been effectively explained to their employees—have usually been pleasantly surprised by the results. Employees, for the most part, have been genuinely involved in making the best choices, and have not changed their minds over and over again, as many had thought they would.

The flexible benefits idea, in short, is no longer something that only the most innovative and daring companies can approach. Now almost anyone can consider flexible benefits without much trepidation.

ALTERNATIVE APPROACHES TO FLEXIBILITY

No matter how attractive the idea of installing a flexible benefits program, it still can be a complicated process. Designing the best program, working out a multitude of details, and, finally, explaining everything to employees may seem like a monumental task. And, all too often, it may *be* such a task. For the solidly established firm, where everyone is reasonably familiar and comfortable with the benefits program, a complete overhaul can be very difficult—even if a radical modernization of that very benefits program is, in truth, long overdue.

So it's not surprising to find that many companies feel flexible benefits make sense, at least in theory, but that a completely flexible program is too much for them to undertake right now. Thus, anything that incorporates the idea of flexibility without requiring a complete change in a company's established benefits structure can be very appealing.

Here are some of the alternatives:

FLEXIBLE SPENDING ACCOUNTS

One small step toward flexibility is the flexible spending account or, to use the inevitable designator, FSA. In essence, an FSA is a sort of mini-flexible benefits device, in which employees are credited each year with an "account" in dollars that they can "spend" as they choose among an array of optional benefits. The money in the account usually comes from one of two sources: It's the employee's own money, put in the account on a pretax or "salary reduction" basis, or it's credited to the employee's account by the company, as financial compensation for having signed up for one of the company's less expensive medical- or life-insurance offerings.

The money can be spent in three ways—according to the IRS regulations published in 1984. It can go for medical expenses not covered by the employee's health plan, especially deductibles or copayments; for a dependent care plan; or for a group legal services plan. Or, if it isn't all spent, it can go to the employee in the form of cash.

It isn't hard to see why free-standing FSAs gained instant popularity. They seemed to be a small venture into flexibility without the pain of organizing a completely flexible benefits program, plus a tax-deferral mechanism. And something else, too: They appeared to offer a real incentive for employees to opt for a cheaper medical insurance plan.

But things were too good to last, it seems. The IRS vetoed the idea of employees' receiving an open-ended account each year and then cashing out their unused balances or rolling them over from year to year. And it decreed that employees must decide, at the beginning of each year, exactly how they planned to spend the money they would have in their accounts. Then, if they guessed wrong, it was simply too bad. The watchword became "use it or lose it."

MODULAR PROGRAMS

Another approach to flexibility is to offer employees alternative assortments, or modules, of benefits. This sort of arrangement is much easier to design and introduce than a *completely* flexible program made up of many individual plans—and choices. Also, it makes employees' decisions much simpler, since they merely select one set of benefits, rather than having to choose them separately from an entire smorgasbord. However, by fitting all benefits into groups, compromises must be made—and the individual employee is less likely to find just the right combination for his or her specific benefits needs.

LIMITED-AREA CHOICES

Even in companies where the very idea of flexible benefits still seems a far-off possibility, flexibility is creeping in. Every time a company offers its employees a selection of medical plans, a choice of life-insurance coverage, or an optional benefit to pay for with their own money, that company is recognizing the value of flexible benefits.

Another way of approaching flexibility, then, is to keep the present program intact but, at periodic intervals, offer a new benefit to be added on, with each employee picking from a list of options. Or employees could have the chance to reduce their level of coverage under one benefit plan in exchange for better coverage under another.

In offering *any* kind of choice, a company is making its benefit program that much more adaptable to the greatly changing needs of its employees.

FLEXIBLE BENEFITS PROGRAMS— SOME EXAMPLES

Flexible benefits programs are not all alike. Some common threads, however, do run through most of the truly flexible programs that have now been put into place. Almost always, for example, employees have a once-a-year opportunity to reappraise their benefits selections and make any changes they wish. And usually they can also have an opportunity to do this when there's a major change in their family situation, such as marriage or the birth of a child.

On the other hand, some important differences will be noticed in the specific details of each program; in most cases, these will concern:

- Whether a fixed core of basic benefits is provided for all employees and, if so, of what this core consists
- The specific flexible benefit areas where an employee may make a choice and the various alternatives that are available
- How the various options may be "paid" for—through benefit credits allocated by the company, a flexible spending account, or out of the employee's own pocket, using either after-tax payroll deductions or pretax ("salary reduction") dollars
- And whether cash payments to the employee are one of the options available

Now let's examine—without going into all the details of each plan—how some individual flexible benefits programs differ from each other, using these (and other) points of reference. And, since they have the longest history—and thus have profited the most from experience—we'll begin with the three pioneer flexible programs: those at TRW, Inc.; the Educational Testing Service; and the American Can Company.

These three programs existed in lonely splendor for a number of years, while other companies observed their fate. Only when these programs seemed to succeed did it become clear that flexible benefits weren't such a bad idea after all. It is interesting to note that, despite their common heritage, these three trailblazing programs were (and still are) quite different from each other.

Finally, in contrast to these three long-established examples, we shall examine the newly introduced program at Thomas Jefferson University in Philadelphia, which might be considered typical of a modern plan that incorporates and builds on what has been learned about flexible benefits as an ongoing process.

TRW, INC.

The first large company to develop a truly flexible benefits program was the TRW Defense and Space Systems Group, with headquarters in Redondo Beach, California. It began on an experimental basis in 1974, and now covers about 11,000 of the firm's salaried and hourly employees in California and a number of other states.

In one sense, the TRW plan is a hybrid—a midpoint between conventional benefits programs and fully flexible ones. It centers around two major benefits: health care and life insurance. Employees are offered a number of options, but all their choices are confined to these areas. Credit obtained by taking a less expensive health plan can only be used for more life insurance or vice versa. However, this program does let an employee make a dramatic choice in balancing life insurance against health care, since it's possible, with either of these two benefits, to pick one plan offering minimal coverage and trade off the credit obtained for quite extensive coverage in the other benefit.

Each November, TRW employees receive a computerized benefit selection worksheet, which lists the charges and credits for all the health-care and life-insurance options. Credits are based on each employee's age, the cost of insurance, and other factors, so they usually change each year. An employee then decides how to trade off between the two benefits, by choosing one health plan and one life insurance option. Any extra charges not covered by credits are paid for via payroll deductions.

If an employee selects one of the low-cost options, the resulting credit must be used for some other benefit—although the company will pay a weekly credit of two dollars or less in cash, if it isn't possible to balance things out exactly.

The TRW flexible program was a genuine breakthrough in offering employees a voice in how they were to be covered by these two important benefits. And follow-up attitude surveys have shown a high level of employee satisfaction with the program.

EDUCATIONAL TESTING SERVICE

The Educational Testing Service, a nonprofit organization with headquarters in Princeton, New Jersey, is by no means a typical American company, but it has become a leader in innovative benefits management. Its flexible benefits program dates back to 1974 and covers more than 2,000 employees, of whom an estimated 40 percent are members of two-earner families.

The ETS flexible benefits program offers a wide range of choices to employees, and it has been in place long enough to have profited from experience and to have made periodic modifications in the options offered. In contrast to many of the more recently adopted programs, ETS provides a broad and complete benefits program to all employees—including comprehensive health-care coverage. After this, the employee can select from a range of extra benefits of his or her choice, without having to "give up" anything.

An employee's total optional benefits credit is equal to a fixed percentage of salary (from 3 to 6 percent, depending on length of service). Each fall, employees receive personal computerized forms listing their current flexible credits (in dollar equivalents), plus the costs of the various options. They can use their allocation of flexible benefits credits to pay for extra life insurance, medical coverage for dependents, dental care, physical exams, a number of retirement or capital-accumulation plans, or additional vacation time. Also, an employee may use salary deductions or, in some cases, pretax dollars, to purchase even more benefits.

Employees may choose to receive in regular monthly payments, any sum ranging from $50 up to the full cash equivalent of all their unused flexible credits in lieu of the benefits these credits could have purchased. Or the entire cash amount for a year can be received in advance on January 15 (with any unearned portion being returnable if an employee leaves the company during the year).

AMERICAN CAN COMPANY

Of the three trailblazers in flexible benefits, the American Can Company has ended up with the kind of program that most closely resembles many of those now appearing throughout the country. It dates back to 1979 and now covers more than 3,000 employees in the company's Greenwich, Connecticut, home office and a number of other locations.

This company offers a core benefit program that provides basic coverage in health care, life insurance, and long-term disability, plus a defined-benefit pension plan. In addition, there is a broad range of health-care and life-insurance options, plus a varied selection of "add-on" benefits. It seems to be meeting employees' needs very well; a survey in 1984 found that 72 percent of them said they were "extremely satisfied" with their benefits.

Each employee receives an annual allotment of flexible benefits credits that varies according to salary and length of service. These credits may be allocated to better medical coverage, dental care, greater LTD, a capital accumulation plan, day care, or additional vacation time. In addition, payroll deductions may be used to purchase all of these except vacation or day care—or to obtain better life insurance and/or AD&D coverage. And, under a 401[k] arrangement, employees may make pretax contributions to the capital-accumulation plan. (There is no cash option.)

To Sum Up

These three pioneer programs have taken three quite different approaches to the flexible benefits concept. One (TRW) offers a broad range of choices, but an employee's options are limited to two major benefits, health care and life insurance. Another (ETS) provides every employee with a comprehensive array of benefits, together with an assortment of optional "extras" to choose from—the classic "cafeteria" idea. And the program of the third company (American Can) has a core of basic benefits for all employees, the possibility of upgrading these benefits, and a number of additional options to choose from as well.

A LATE-MODEL PROGRAM: THOMAS JEFFERSON UNIVERSITY

Building on what was learned at TRW, Educational Testing Service, and American Can Company—as well as at other firms that ventured cautiously into flexible benefits in the early 1980s—an increasing number of companies have recently joined the movement. Although several consulting firms have developed standardized flexible benefits systems, the concept is still so new that most companies are finding that their program ends up as something unique—something that is best suited to that company's own special business situation and, especially, its own mix of people. And this, of course, is all to the good, since that's exactly what a flexible benefits system is supposed to do.

However, despite this disclaimer, it may be useful to take a more extensive look at one company's newly introduced flexible benefits program to see how it differs from the three prototypes we have been discussing. For this purpose, we shall use OPT, the flexible benefits program that was introduced in 1984 to the 3,800 nonbargaining unit staff members of Thomas Jefferson University, a prominent medical school in Philadelphia.

The plan in brief

The OPT program offers employees a wide selection of optional benefits choices (including a flexible spending account)—or, if they prefer, the opportunity to keep all benefits at the same levels they were before October 1, 1984, when the new flexible benefits program went into effect.

Basic core benefits

Benefits without flexible features include retirement plans, dental and vision care, tuition assistance, and vacation. In addition, these standard benefits are provided as a minimum to all employees:

- *Life insurance.* An amount equal to 150 percent (for faculty and senior administrators), 100 percent (for house staff), or 50 percent (for all other employees) of annual base salary, up to a maximum of $50,000, plus an equal amount of AD&D protection.
- *Short-term disability.* Salary continuation up to 26 weeks for faculty and senior staff, 12 annual sick days for other employees.
- *Long-term disability.* After 180 days of total disability, LTD benefits of 50 percent of base salary; minimum $50, maximum $6,000 (including payments from other sources).

Benefits choices

- *Medical insurance.*
  1. A comprehensive Blue Cross/Blue Shield plan with a $250-per-person deductible, which then pays 100 percent

of semiprivate room charges for 120 days plus 80 percent of "reasonable and customary" surgical bills. Major medical follows, also with a $250 individual deductible, paying 80 percent of covered expenses up to a $10,000 out-of-pocket limit, then 100 percent.

2. A high-option plan, providing hospital services for 120 days and 100 percent of usual and customary surgical fees, with no deductible, together with major medical paying 100 percent of covered expenses after a $100 individual deductible.

3. A "dual coverage" plan (open only to employees covered by another family member's medical insurance), which pays 25 percent of all usual, customary, and reasonable expenses after a $100 deductible, up to the $10,000 out-of-pocket maximum.

4. As an alternative, an employee may choose from six available health maintenance organizations.

- *Life insurance.* Any of five optional amounts, ranging up to four times base annual salary can be added onto the core benefit; this can be supplemented by extra AD&D protection in $10,000 units up to a maximum of $500,000. In addition, there is a choice of three levels of dependent life insurance.
- *Short-term disability.* Three options (only for employees not eligible for salary continuation): (1) payments equal to 66 2/3 percent of salary with a maximum of $165 per week plus the possibility of supplementing this amount with partial sick days; (2) 66 2/3 percent with no maximum limit; or (3) 80 percent with no maximum.
- *Long-term disability.* Two choices are possible, each having the same provisions as the core LTD plan, but paying either 60 percent or 70 percent of base salary instead of 50 percent.
- *Spending account.* This can be used to pay for medical bills not covered by the employee's medical-insurance plan, dependent-care expenses, dental or vision care, or personal legal expenses—all out of pretax income.

Payment for optional benefits
When the plan was inaugurated, all eligible employees received an allotment of benefit credits, depending on their age, salary, and dependent status. These represented the difference in the biweekly cost of the new core benefit program and the university's pre-October 1, 1984, benefits program. They could use these to obtain any of the higher-level benefits; using the exact amount of credits would mean keeping benefits at the pre-OPT level. Then, this allotment could be supplemented by pretax ("salary reduction") contributions, up to a specified biweekly maximum amount, to obtain any extra benefits. (Under this plan, employees are not permitted to make after-tax deductions).

From then on, employees may make a new set of choices each year, or when "special life events" (such as change in marital status) occur.

Cash option
The cash value of any unused benefit credits can be received as part of the employee's regular biweekly paycheck, if desired.

WHAT ABOUT THE FUTURE OF FLEXIBLE BENEFITS?

A very good question. Despite the worrisome problem of taxation of flexible benefits, the underlying reasoning for flexibility won't go away. The employees who work for a company will continue to be more diverse and heterogeneous—with a wider array of benefits needs. And, if a company wants to provide them with any benefits at all, it makes little sense to try to fit every employee into the same rigid box.

So an optimist must assume that the inevitable ingenuity of benefits people will prevail. Despite the jaundiced eye that government may cast at the lush table of "cafeteria" benefits, new approaches will be designed—ones that can avoid the onus of seeming to give an unfair advantage to the fortunate employees of some companies. Perhaps broad-based flexible benefits programs will never attain the instant popularity of the Section 401[k] plan or the free-standing flexible spending account. But, in the long run, they may help employee benefits adapt to the world of the future.

4
SOME IMPORTANT BENEFITS ISSUES

In Chapter 2 we discussed some of the more important benefits questions that have arisen recently, such as how to contain the rising costs of health care, the increasing interest in defined-contribution retirement plans and how this will affect the traditional defined-benefit plan, and the future of Social Security. Here we shall be concerned with a number of equally important issues, but ones that are more general in nature—reaching across the boundaries among individual benefit plans.

For each of these issues, we have organized the material into a standard format: first, some background information; then the chief arguments for and against a controversial position; and, finally, some educated guesses as to what may happen in the future. In every case, we have attempted to present the arguments on both sides of each issue in as fair a way as possible.

WHAT WILL HAPPEN IF BENEFITS ARE TAXED MORE HEAVILY?

Perhaps this question should really be, "What will happen *when* benefits are taxed more heavily?" At present, it's still too early to know how many of the proposed reforms of the federal income tax system will actually become law—especially those proposals that would include some formerly tax-free benefits in an employee's taxable income. It seems most unlikely that the Congress will ever enact legislation making the majority of benefits taxable. But, on the other hand, it seems virtually certain that some kinds of benefits that heretofore have gone tax free will not escape the IRS forever.

We shall, therefore, try to discuss the issue in general terms, without assuming that the tax status of any specific benefit will change. Some fundamental principles must first be dealt with—ideas that are central to the concept of employee benefits. It is particularly important for anyone who is concerned with benefits to understand both sides of this question. Strong voices favor taxing benefits, and the opposition must deal logically with the arguments that will be raised—both now and in the future.

BACKGROUND

Some people in the benefits community were more surprised than they should have been when the Department of the Treasury made its first tax-reform proposals in 1984. After all, the taxation of benefits is not something entirely new. In discussing various individual benefit plans in Chapter 2, we mentioned a number of ways in which benefits have long been treated by the tax laws. Cash disbursements from profit-sharing plans, premiums on life insurance above the $50,000 level, reimbursements for some kinds of relocation and education expenses, and a number of executive perquisites have long been considered taxable income for those who received them.

And the income from every kind of retirement plan—pension, profit sharing, or whatever—has never been tax free; taxes have simply been deferred until the benefits were actually received. Even the traditional tax-free status of Social Security benefits has now been curtailed for some people. Nor should anyone forget that every employee's annual "contribution" to Social Security—amounting to several thousand dollars—is made from *after-tax* income.

However, it has long been accepted that most of the major employee benefits—health insurance, basic life insurance, and the like—would not be considered part of an employee's taxable income. And many benefit plans have taken their present form for the very reason that the tax laws were as they were. Now that could change. Ever since the original tax proposals, the benefits community has been working strenuously to stave off the potential threat of federal taxation.

However, the outlook has not been improved by some benefits professionals—particularly those who have been loud in praising the tax advantages of, for example, Section 401[k] plans, and much softer in talking about the less-exciting benefits that offer much-needed protection to a broad group of employees.

The Treasury and its supporters have argued strongly in favor of its new philosophy, and the benefits community has answered in equal force. The two sides to this vitally important question can be summarized in this general fashion:

THE ARGUMENTS *FOR* BENEFITS TAXATION

- Benefits represent a large, virtually untapped source of revenue. In its proposed overhauling of the federal income tax system, the Treasury suggested a number of radical changes, many of which involved eliminating deductions or levying entirely new taxes. The benefits-taxation proposal is part of the second group. The government, having observed the remarkable growth of employee benefits over the years, felt that the benefits received by employees were really part of their compensation—and should be taxed.

- Benefits are distributed unequally. In justifying its taxation proposals, the Treasury developed a concept of "horizontal equity." The implication is that anything that is not received by all taxpayers almost universally represents an unfair financial benefit to those who do get it—and thus should be taxed, so that this advantage is reduced. And, since some people pay income tax but don't have employer-paid benefits plans—the self-employed, for example—it's unfair for other people to receive benefits without paying taxes on them.

THE ARGUMENTS *AGAINST* BENEFITS TAXATION

- Benefits make a significant contribution to the nation's welfare. If private employee benefit plans were not in force, the government would have to step in to fill the void. How else would employees be protected against possible disasters like death, disability, and serious illness? Without company-paid benefits, a great many workers couldn't afford to buy individual insurance coverage—or would simply take their chances of not needing it. And those with low risks would be the most likely to do so, thus increasing the premium cost for those who remained. The expense of a national health-insurance program or the like would be tremendous. Thus, it's unfair that employee benefits, which lift a large financial burden from the government's shoulders, should be penalized through taxation.
- A benefit premium may not represent a tangible benefit. It's unfair, for example, to pay taxes on the annual premiums that your employer paid to a medical plan when you haven't been sick during the year and thus haven't received any financial benefits from that plan. This is changing the rules of the game: Traditionally, taxes are only due when you actually receive some kind of financial gain.

WHAT COULD HAPPEN?

It's difficult to believe that all traditional employee benefits will ever be taxed; even the Treasury's original proposals spared some of the basic core of benefits, such as a portion of the premiums for health insurance. On the other hand, it seems inevitable that benefits will never be completely free of the possibilities of new taxation.

With this in mind, therefore, it may be a useful exercise to make some educated guesses about what the effects of taxes on benefits might be. Here are two possible courses of action:

- A company will decide to cut back radically on its benefits programs. This may be especially likely for a firm that has always been conservative in its approach to employee benefits and has never been very enthusiastic about providing any more than the bare essentials. The new tax laws may be all it needs to convince itself that it was right all along.
- A company will make no changes at all in its benefits program. Assuming it believes strongly in the value of benefits for their own sake, not for their tax advantages, the company will be very reluctant to change its mind. It may even decide to provide employees with increases in salary to offset any additional tax liabilities.

For most companies, of course, the choice will be somewhere between these two positions; perhaps keeping most of its present benefits, but being very reluctant to add anything new, or perhaps developing entirely new kinds of benefits programs that can operate within the framework of the new tax laws—whatever they may be.

SHOULD EMPLOYEES PAY MORE OF THE COSTS?

With the rapid increase in the cost of almost all employee benefits, it is not surprising to hear it suggested that employees themselves should share more of the burden. Why should employers pay so much of the bills, the argument goes, especially when there is increasing danger that some of this expense may not be tax deductible in the future?

BACKGROUND

In the early days of employee benefits—before today's pattern of company-paid plans had been established—it was not uncommon to find employers who paid very little of the costs of their employees' benefits. A company might offer its employees the opportunity to take advantage of a group medical-insurance plan, such as Blue Cross, and a group life-insurance plan—but not contribute very much, if anything, toward the monthly premiums out of its own pocket. Many of the retirement plans then in force also required employee contributions.

Of course, the premiums for all of these benefits were usually quite modest by today's standards, both in real dollars and as a percentage of salary.

In later years, however, the tide began to turn. For a number of logical reasons, companies found themselves paying a much greater portion of the costs of benefits—especially health insurance.

Competitive pressures became very strong. As more and more companies established various kinds of benefit plans, it became difficult for others not to do likewise, especially if they were competing for the same pool of employees. And labor unions were able to gain significant increases in company-paid benefits provided for their members. For a while, benefits moved onward and upward without much of a pause. Companies added on one new kind of benefit after another to their programs—and many of these new additions came completely free to employees.

Also, as the costs of benefits went up, many companies that had been sharing premiums with their employees were reluctant to pass on increases every time they occurred—so that the companies' percentage of the shared expense grew faster than the amount contributed by employees.

But the honeymoon had to end sometime. With benefits expenses rising to unexpected heights at the same time that the business boom began to slow, rapid expansion of benefits programs came to an end. Instead, by the early 1980s it was much more common to see companies cut back on their benefits than to broaden them. Even the unions reluctantly curtailed their campaigns for new and better benefits—concentrating, instead, on holding on to what they had already gained.

For a company that is feeling strong financial pressures to limit its benefits expense, however, it is very difficult to eliminate a benefit plan entirely. Once a plan is in effect, employees feel that it is something that is owed to them—and they will never gladly accept its disappearance. An easier solution, then, is for a company to retain all its benefit plans—but to increase the share of the cost that employees must pay. As we pointed out earlier, many of the "cost-containment" schemes that companies have incorporated into their health-insurance plans—such as larger deductibles and coinsurance percentages—are actually means of shifting some of the cost burden from the company to its employees. Of course, these are never popular. But companies have discovered, sometimes to their surprise, that many employees, once they understand the full cost picture, would rather pay more for a valuable benefit like health insurance than see its coverage reduced in any way.

THE ARGUMENTS *FOR* INCREASING EMPLOYEES' SHARE OF COSTS

- It's the only fair thing to do. As benefits costs go up, it makes sense for both employees and their company to share equally in the added expense.
- Some employees have no need for a particular benefit, so why should a company spend a lot of money providing

them with it? If people actually want a certain benefit, they shouldn't mind paying for part of its cost—or even all of it.

THE ARGUMENTS *AGAINST* INCREASING EMPLOYEES' SHARE OF COSTS

- The extra cost will be hardest on those at the lowest end of the pay scale, which may force them, if they have the option, to pass up benefits they really need to protect their families. Does a company want the responsibility for this?
- It will lead to adverse selection: Those least likely to receive payments under a plan will be the first to opt out, thus increasing the overall risk for those who remain. And this will eventually push insurance premiums even higher.

WHAT COULD HAPPEN?

Most companies still feel that it is their obligation to protect employees from major disasters, which means they will probably be quite reluctant to do anything that would leave someone's family in real financial distress because of serious illness, permanent disability, or death. So it will be the benefits that deal with less serious occurrences—such as dental plans, tuition reimbursement, and the like—that will probably be the first targets for any cost-sharing moves.

And the argument that it's wasteful for a company to spend money on benefits that employees don't really want can be countered, to large extent, by adopting a flexible benefits program of some sort (as described in Chapter 3). In this way, the company can decide exactly how much it wants to spend on benefits, and its employees can decide how they want their share to be allocated.

IS EVERYONE ENTITLED TO THE SAME BENEFITS?

On the surface, the answer would seem to be, "Of course they are." But closer examination of this question may lead to a different answer today.

BACKGROUND

In the good old American democratic tradition, one might expect a company to provide the same benefits for one and all. And many companies maintain the pleasant fiction that this is indeed the case. However, except for those very small companies that can still afford to operate on a share-and-share-alike basis, it's very rare to find true equality in the way that benefits are allocated.

As soon as a firm gets large enough to have distinct employee groups, it becomes increasingly likely that one group will receive benefits that differ from those of another group. These distinctions all depend on a company's individual structure, such as: exempt vs. nonexempt employees; hourly vs. salaried; union vs. nonunion; line vs. staff; head office vs. branches; sales vs. nonsales; management vs. non-management. (But one distinction that has *almost* completely disappeared: male vs. female.)

Sometimes this distinction will be all too apparent—such as a prominent executive dining room or special parking area. Other benefits differences, however, may not be visible to the naked eye, but be buried in the recesses of a benefit plan's formal text. For example, a retirement plan might state that pensions are to be determined by a person's "final average *base pay*." This would yield much different results for an outside salesman whose income at retirement was $20,000 in salary plus an average of $20,000 in commissions, as compared with a sales manager who received a flat $40,000 in base salary.

Also, when a company pays all or part of family medical insurance, it is obviously providing a much more valuable—and more expensive—benefit to someone with a spouse and five children than to a single employee.

Other benefits distinctions may arise because of plans' eligibility rules, which can include age minimums and maximums or waiting periods before new employees are covered by a particular plan. Age requirements are succumbing rapidly to new legislation, but length-of-service requirements for eligibility still remain in many plans.

These waiting periods are most likely to be found in such

areas as profit sharing, thrift plans, vacation, and sick days than in benefits that provide protection against catastrophe, such as life insurance and medical plans. And the longest waiting period—10 years—is the one that most employees must complete before they are finally vested and eligible for a pension under a company's typical defined-benefit retirement plan.

These kinds of differences are long established, and they usually are accepted (although sometimes grudgingly) by most employees. And the government keeps a close watch (more so today than ever before) over any benefit plans in which out-and-out discrimination seems possible.

But the issue now arises of making further benefits distinctions *within* employee groups. As we saw in our discussions of individual benefits in Chapter 2, pension plans and long-term disability insurance, by their very definitions, are directly tied to salary level. And the same can be said for group life insurance. So the question might be asked: Why stop there? Why not base some of the other common benefits on salary level, also? (Some of the new flexible benefits plans are doing exactly that.)

This reasoning, of course, runs in two directions. If you think of benefits primarily as *rewards*, you might consider giving a higher level of benefits—such as a longer vacation or a larger matching percentage for the company's contribution to a savings plan—to recognize good job performance. On the other hand, if you think of benefits as being based on real *needs*, it might be argued that employees at higher pay levels could better afford larger deductibles or greater out-of-pocket maximums in their medical insurance.

THE ARGUMENTS *FOR* MORE DISTINCTIONS IN BENEFITS

- Since benefits are really part of total compensation, they should be treated like other forms of compensation—with greater amounts going to those who earn them by performing best.

- It doesn't make sense to give new employees the full array of benefits right from the start. There's a lot of administrative work involved in signing up everyone for all the plans, and many of these people will quit in the first few months anyway.

THE ARGUMENTS *AGAINST* MORE DISTINCTIONS IN BENEFITS

- Real needs, in many cases, do not depend on salary level or length of service. The situation is bad enough as it is—particularly in the case of life insurance. The best idea is not to second-guess an individual's requirements, but to provide the identical set of benefits to everyone within a broad group of employees.
- Giving benefits as rewards for performance may be appealing at first glance, but what do you do when an employee's performance slips? Taking away a counted-on benefit could be much more traumatic than necessary.

WHAT COULD HAPPEN?

First of all, with the increasing use of electronic data processing in human resources administration, the increased-paperwork argument (for not adding new employees to benefit plan rolls) would seem to be less valid than it may once have been.

Using benefit levels as part of a system of rewards is a relatively new idea, and there's not much concrete evidence upon which to judge its effectiveness. However, if such a scheme were used as part of a conventional benefits program, it wouldn't be applied to benefits life insurance or long-term disability, which are intended to fend off disasters that could strike anyone, regardless of job performance.

However, the use of flexible benefits arrangements such as those outlined in Chapter 3 offers a possible way to incorporate differing levels of benefits into a compensation system. Under such a program, each employee is given a total amount of overall benefits—in the form of credits or actual dollar costs—to be allocated as he or she chooses. But there's no reason why this total must be the same for everyone. It's quite feasible for a company to vary it according to any guidelines it may choose—years of service, employment level, or job performance. The negative aspects of having distinctions in benefits between two groups of employees, or within the same group, will be much less apparent in this sort of arrangement. Under a flexible plan, after all, everyone ends up with a different combination of benefits anyway.

WHAT ABOUT POST-RETIREMENT BENEFITS?

Many companies may feel that most of their responsibility to any employee ends once that person has retired. However, in recent years there has been growing pressure for continuing a limited amount of employee benefits coverage throughout retirement.

BACKGROUND
It was not too long ago that most employees who reached age 65 simply went on the pension rolls and, except possibly for a retirees' newsletter or a Christmas letter from the chairman, all formal ties to their old company came to an end.

In many cases, that's still what happens. However, a number of significant trends in recent years have caused some companies to reappraise their traditional treatment of their retired employees. First of all, the country's total retired population is growing rapidly—a result of improving health among the elderly and a trend toward retirement at an earlier age. For a large and long-established firm, its own retirement population will reflect this same dramatic growth.

This trend will continue—and have a growing impact on all companies except those with a young staff that is still a long way from retirement. Ironically, a mature company that is forced to make stringent staff reductions to maintain its financial stability will be particularly hard hit, since one of the most popular ways to reduce excess personnel is to persuade, somehow, as many people as possible to take early retirement.

Pressure has come from another direction, too. The rising cost of living has had its effects on the retired population, along with everyone else. And it's not illogical for a retiree to seek relief from his or her former employer—the one who's been sending those pension checks that seem to buy less and less each month.

Many retired employees continue to be covered by a modest amount of group life insurance (usually sharply reduced from what they had while actively employed) and some other relatively minor benefits. But the major pressure will come in two most important areas: health insurance and pensions.

At one time, it seemed that Medicare might take care of almost all the medical expenses of the country's retired population, but that, unfortunately, seems to have been much too optimistic a hope. Medicare's financial difficulties, as is all too well known, have been brought about by the demographic factors we have mentioned, along with the sharp rise in almost all health care costs. To keep the program relatively solvent, changes in its benefits structure have been put into effect—and it won't be surprising to see even more radical changes in Medicare in years to come.

The Medicare changes—both those already enacted and those likely for the future—take several forms. However, the effect of almost all of them will be the same: Retirees will have to pay more out of their own pockets for medical care. So there will be increasing pressure on those companies that have not continued medical insurance for their retirees to do so. (In fact, many states now require that *all* terminated employees—not just those who retire—must have the opportunity to purchase health insurance coverage at group rates.) And there will be equally strong pressure for retirees' health insurance to provide much broader coverage—at a much higher cost to the companies. Also, under a recent court ruling, once a company has begun continuing benefits to retirees, it cannot arbitrarily cut them off.

Retirees' medical-insurance plans usually include a "carve-out" provision so that the plan won't give duplicate benefits for things covered by Medicare—and this carve-out seems destined to get smaller in size in years to come.

Pensions present a somewhat different problem. Here, the government program is in much better shape. Social Security, for the moment at least, seems to have reached a state of financial stability. And, even with the changes made in 1983, retirees receiving Social Security benefits can count on regular cost-of-living increases in their payments—although these are a frequent target of governmental budget-balancing proposals.

The same, unfortunately, cannot be said for their private pension-plan checks. And this is especially true for those people who retired under defined-benefit plans that calculated lifetime pensions on salaries that had been earned in preinflation days. What once seemed reasonably generous has greatly diminished in purchasing power.

Very few, if any, company retirement plans include automatic provisions for cost-of-living increases in retirees' pensions, like those incorporated into the Social Security program. But many companies have, at intervals over the years, decided to make upward adjustments to the pensions they have been paying to retirees. These increases have usually been made *ad hoc*—based almost entirely on a company's current financial health or feelings of altruism. And, as the inflationary spiral continues (even though the dramatic inflation of the 1970s has been reduced) and more and more people continue to retire with defined-benefit pensions, the pressure to grant additional increases in the size of pensions will continue.

THE ARGUMENTS *FOR* EXPANDING POST-RETIREMENT BENEFITS

- It's a company's duty to take care of its retirees, and it's particularly poor public relations to leave these people

completely on their own. After all, they contributed many years of service to their company and had expected to retire without many worries about their finances. Why should they be left to the cruel mercies of an inflationary spiral no one had anticipated?
- If private industry does nothing for the retired population, there will be growing demands for someone else to act. The increasing numbers of retirees, most of whom vote regularly, can create political pressures for solutions that most companies would not welcome—such as mandatory cost-of-living increases in pensions or compulsory health insurance for retirees.

THE ARGUMENTS *AGAINST* EXPANDING POST-RETIREMENT BENEFITS

- A company has enough problems in providing suitable benefits for its active employees, without worrying about those who retired years ago. It's too bad that they have been hit hard by inflation, but that's something no one could have expected.
- Many retired employees may actually be better off than they were while actively working, especially those who have been prudent in handling their financial affairs and invested their money wisely. And today's retirees are also receiving benefits from Social Security and Medicare that far exceed the relatively small amounts they contributed to those plans. So any across-the-board company contributions for retirees' benefits might very well be money wasted on many people who really don't need it. It's much better to operate on a year-by-year basis as the situation requires.

WHAT COULD HAPPEN?

As always, it's almost impossible to make predictions about the future of the country's economy. If inflation returns to the levels of the late 1970s and early 1980s, demands for financial relief for the retired population will certainly increase.

However, there is a very real possibility that retirees' defined-benefit pensions that are paid in fixed-dollar amounts will inevitably become—gradually or quickly—less valuable in terms of real dollars. Whether a company decides to do anything about this will be its own decision.

HOW SHOULD A BENEFIT PLAN BE FUNDED?

Today many companies must face this decision: Who should have ultimate financial responsibility for an employee benefits program—an outside organization or the company itself?

BACKGROUND

In the early days of employee benefits, it was customary for most major plans to be handled exclusively by insurance companies, accounting firms, benefits consultants, banks, investment managers, and similar outside organizations. Together, they shared the responsibility for designing and administering benefits plans; providing pooled-funding arrangements; supervising trust funds; paying claims; and even supplying all the necessary forms, booklets, and other printed material. A company simply paid the bills.

In a sense, this made everything much simpler—if more expensive. And, for a small company, there is still no other practical course of action. However, many larger firms have discovered that there are a number of advantages to taking on some of the work that once had been the exclusive property of outsiders.

Among the first to go was the individual insurance policy

purchased to finance each employee's retirement income. And, as the vast trust funds supporting the new pension funds began to accumulate, many companies began to feel that they could manage this money as well as any outside investment manager could.

As time has passed, companies have begun to see the advantages (despite the headaches involved) of taking over other aspects of benefit plans—such as employee communications and claims processing. After all, there are many attractions to eliminating the middleman. But the ultimate move is self-funding—taking on the actual financial responsibility for a particular benefit. In effect, this means operating as one's own insurance company.

In recent years, there has been a dramatic increase in the number of companies that are self-funding their medical benefits. It has been estimated that more than half of all employers are now doing so to some extent.

However, legal restrictions may sometimes get in the way of self-funding. At first glance, it might seem sensible for a company to avoid the middleman and set up its own life insurance arrangement—especially if the firm is large enough to take best advantage of the laws of probability that govern life and death. There wouldn't be the expense of regular premiums to an insurance company—they would just have to be prepared to pay out a fixed sum to the survivors whenever an active employee died. Unfortunately, it isn't that simple. To the government, this scheme smacks of tax avoidance, and thus various rules and regulations make self-funding of life insurance almost impossible.

One development that has furthered the trend toward self-funding of employee benefit plans has been the use of tax-exempt trusts, commonly known as Section 501(c)(9) trusts or voluntary employees' beneficiary associations (VEBAs). Not really "associations," they're simply paper organizations that are set up, within certain prescribed legal guidelines, to act as tax-exempt financial conduits for funding almost any kind of employee benefit plan.

THE ARGUMENTS *FOR* SELF-FUNDING
- It saves money. In most cases, the internal administrative costs will be less than the fees and commissions that must be paid to an outside organization. Also, cash flow is improved, since a company is only charged for claims when they actually occur, rather than having to pay premiums in advance. And, in some cases, a self-funded benefit plan is exempt from state taxes on insurance premiums.
- Claims can be handled more efficiently. Many companies feel they know their own people much better than any outside organization ever could, and that eliminating the middleman will cut out a lot of administrative paperwork and make any errors easier to correct.

THE ARGUMENTS *AGAINST* SELF-FUNDING
- The risks may be too great. A large insurance firm spreads the risks, and can anticipate its total claims on the basis of broad experience. A single company, however, is putting all its eggs in one basket; annual costs are much harder to gauge—and an unexpected disaster could be very costly. (Although self-insured plans usually take the precaution of stop-loss protection against major claims.)
- Administration may be more costly than expected. Most companies are not in the insurance business, and may not have the experience to evaluate unusual claims or unexpected situations. Special accounting problems may arise, and a company could even be liable for damage suits if errors were made.

WHAT COULD HAPPEN?
The attractions of possible cost savings will always induce companies to investigate new ideas—and self-funding of benefits certainly fits that description. The chief problem is simply one of size; until a company is large enough to make self-funding economically viable, it must rely on outside help.

Outside organizations cannot be expected to let business slip out of their hands without a fight. They are constantly offering new insurance products and new computerized administrative systems that, they hope, will make self-funding less attractive. Another possible hazard may be the increased attention that the VEBA device is receiving from the Treasury, which apparently views it as one more tax-avoidance scheme to be curtailed with tougher restrictions and regulations.

5
MANAGING EMPLOYEE BENEFITS

Until now, we have been talking about individual employee-benefit plans as separate entities. But no plan stands alone. All must work together as part of an employee-benefits *program*—a program that, taken as a carefully designed package of benefits, will do the best possible job for a particular company and its own mix of employees.

No matter how carefully a benefits program is put together, it cannot be engraved in stone. Companies change; the economy changes; people change. And benefits must change to adapt to these changing circumstances. That doesn't necessarily mean that new plans must constantly be added or that established plans must go through a continual process of amendment. Rather, an employee-benefits program must be efficiently managed to make sure that it responds to all the changes that will inevitably occur. Simply minding the store isn't enough.

Every company's benefits program is unique; not surprisingly, since each company's business objectives, methods of operation, special "culture," and geographical location will produce a combination unlike any other.

However, some general principles can be established and discussed. In this chapter we shall discuss some of these principles, and in Chapter 6 we shall turn our attention to one broad area of management—benefits communication.

KEEPING UP TO DATE

A company's benefits program doesn't exist in a vacuum. Many outside influences will have important effects on its operation. Good management of any benefits program must involve an awareness of these influences, and then dealing with every new situation that arises. Among these influences are:

The competition
When one company makes a major change in its benefits program, the news quickly spreads. Even before the official announcement, word of mouth may already have broadcast its details to employees of other companies. (This is most likely to occur, of course, in tight-knit industries or small communities, where everyone seems to know what everyone else is doing.) Immediately the questions will begin: "Why aren't we getting that benefit, too?"

The benefits community
Employee benefits has become a major industry. Its practitioners include companies that specialize in benefits consulting as well as many of the established insurance, accounting, and management-consulting firms. Anyone who is interested in adding, changing, improving, or replacing a benefits plan can get a great deal of help from these companies. Selecting the best one can often be a difficult task, and, to be realistic, the ultimate choice is often based on personal relationships rather than careful analysis of what various consultants may actually have to offer.

Of course, most outside firms are not completely impartial.

They do have products to sell, and what they say sometimes must be judged accordingly. However, it's the business of benefits consultants to be in touch with what's going on—and thus they almost always are excellent sources of up-to-date information.

The government
For good or bad, governmental bodies at all levels have begun to focus increased attention on employee benefits. The passage of ERISA (the Employees' Retirement Income Security Act of 1974) was a watershed in the interest of government in benefits. And, in 1984, many benefits people who had had their heads in the sand were surprised when the Treasury proposed extensive restrictions on the previously tax-free status of many benefits.

A benefits manager must monitor carefully the possibility—or reality—of government intervention. Laws are being passed; regulations are being issued; decisions are being made by the courts. The paper chase is constant: Forms must be filled out and submitted; reports must be filed; and the like. Keeping abreast of governmental requirements is almost a full-time occupation.

The economy
Employee benefits, finally, are influenced by the changing conditions in the economy itself. We have seen, for instance, what a dramatic effect the rising cost of health care has had on health-insurance premiums. And the relationship works in the opposite direction as well. Pension plans, as a group, are the largest single investor in the American economy today.

This interdependence between the economy and employee benefits means that one cannot change without affecting the other. A change in the ways in which pension plans decide to invest their money can have a major influence on the stock market. And, simultaneously, a strong economic trend, either upward or downward, can have an important effect on the direction that a company's benefits policy will take.

GETTING FEEDBACK

One of the most serious mistakes benefits managers can make is to look at things from only their own point of view. After all, what we're talking about are *employee* benefits, and, unless a company is very well aware of how its employees feel about their benefits, it will be working completely in the dark.

This is true whatever your basic attitude toward employee benefits may be: If you think of benefits primarily as a means of satisfying needs, you must know exactly what your employees' needs are. Or, if you consider benefits to be more in the nature of rewards, you must know what kinds of benefits your employees really want, if these rewards are to have any meaning to them.

Benefits managers, unfortunately, sometimes seem to operate in their own little universe. They talk to each other, to benefits consultants, and to their counterparts in other companies. Unfortunately, they seem not to talk to employees in their own company. And that can be a serious mistake. Who else but the people concerned are the best sources of information about a company's benefits program?

There are many ways of keeping in touch. The following are probably the most effective.

Opinion and attitude surveys

The most systematic means of finding out what employees think about their company's benefits program is to undertake a formal survey. Although easy to propose, a survey, unfortunately, isn't always as easy a solution as if first may seem to be. In fact, a survey that's hastily put together and badly designed can result in misleading or inaccurate information—and actually make matters worse.

But here are some guidelines for getting accurate answers:

- Go into the whole process with an open mind. Don't just use a survey to support some preconceived notion. If the results are radically different from what you anticipated, pay attention to them.

- Don't be amateurish. It's simple enough just to insert a benefits questionnaire in the employee newspaper and wait for the results. But what you get back may be virtually useless: You'll have no idea whether the people who replied are representative of the total employee population. To get accurate results, you don't need a large number of answers, but they *must* be a truly random sample. Obtain professional assistance in selecting that sample.
- Word your questions carefully. Don't just ask people whether they like or don't like a certain benefit plan; make them tell you more. Such devices as ranking benefits in order of preference or dividing up a fixed sum of benefits dollars among various plans can provide more useful information.
- Recognize the impact of a survey itself. Despite anything you say, many employees will be suspicious of any questions they are asked. They'll be much more likely to give frank answers if a questionnaire is anonymous. And the very fact that a survey is being undertaken will have an effect on the employees who participate. If nothing happens as a result, this effect will definitely be negative.

Panel discussions and focus groups

No matter how carefully it is designed, a printed questionnaire always has limitations. It's a cold, formal device, and it raises resistance among many people. For that reason, and because no questionnaire can really pry much below the surface of peoples' attitudes—about employee benefits or anything else—many companies prefer to use a series of small group discussions. Often called "focus groups," these can yield valuable information that is not revealed by a simple questionnaire.

Here it's also important that participants in the group discussions be a representative sampling of the whole employee population. The meetings must be carefully structured and supervised, so that they cover the intended subjects for discussion and don't degenerate into general gripe sessions. Obviously, this is another case where amateurism must be avoided; running an effective focus-group meeting is a job for a skilled professional.

Upward communications systems
Sometimes the best information about employee attitudes toward a benefits program arrives all by itself. Many companies already have some means of upward employee communications (and, if they don't, they probably should have one). If this employee "hot line," anonymous question-and-answer column, or whatever begins to be filled with puzzled inquiries and seemingly justifiable complaints about benefits, it's time to take notice.

Informal channels
Feedback will often come from unexpected directions. An alert benefits manager can become aware of problems—current or potential—from a number of informal sources. It can be almost anything: a lot of errors in filling out a new medical form, comments about benefits during exit interviews with departing employees, false rumors that gain wide circulation, and so on. Any one of these may provide some interesting insights into employees' true feelings about their benefits—ones that a more formal communications mechanism don't always reveal.

PLANNING AHEAD

Now, assuming that you've obtained—in one way or another—what seems to be a pretty accurate reading of your employees' attitude about their benefits program, what are you going do about it all? An employee-benefits program, as we have tried to make clear, can never be something that a company sets up and then forgets about. It takes careful planning to make certain that a company's benefits keep abreast of changing times and shifting conditions.

Establishing overall goals

Planning, of course, must begin at the beginning; and this may mean going back to the very reasons why a company initiated an employee-benefits program. As we outlined in Chapter 1, these reasons can differ greatly from company to company; it is never a single, simple answer.

One company's benefits policy will be influenced by the view that, at heart, benefits only exist in response to a company's duty to supply certain *needs* for protection against unexpected disasters. Another company will consider benefits as part of an employee's total compensation, which is received as a *reward* for services rendered.

Very few companies will look at benefits entirely from either of these viewpoints; each will feel they both are important to a certain extent. But each company's benefits program will take its overall shape under the influence of the relative strength of needs and rewards.

Within that general framework, a company must decide:

- what its *goals* are;
- what kinds of *benefits* will accomplish those goals; and
- what specific benefit *plans* will do that job best.

This might be called a functional approach to benefits management.

Meshing company goals and employee attitudes

In a perfect world, employees' wants and management's needs would be identical. That would make employee-benefits planning very easy. But, to be realistic, in only the rarest of cases will employees and management have the same feelings about benefits. For one thing, employees, as we have pointed out, do not speak with one voice. A genuinely "typical" employee does not exist; even with the best internal communication, the most a company can do is to discover what a majority of its people may want.

So, in the end, planning a benefits program must involve the thoughtful meshing of (a) a company's basic philosophy about the objectives of benefits, together with the specific benefit plans that will achieve these goals and (b) the attitudes of its employees toward the benefits they receive. Any company, if it wants to, is certainly free to ignore employee attitudes completely—and some do exactly that. But most firms will probably find that this is not the most intelligent way to plan a benefits program, especially with the tremendous costs that are involved today.

Developing long-range plans

Planning for the long range can easily involve fundamental changes in a company's approach to benefits. As we explained in Chapter 3, it may mean moving toward a system of flexible benefits. And such a step can easily require a whole series of changes in individual benefit plans.

Long-range planning may simply involve the introduction of an entirely new benefit, such as a dental plan or company-paid long-term disability insurance; or the introduction of a series of measures to contain health-care costs; or the replacement of one major benefit plan by a another, such as substituting a defined-contribution retirement scheme for a defined-benefit pension plan.

Planning all the ramifications of one of these changes can be a major task, but the work will not end there. Changes in one benefit may well mean that it is appropriate to make changes in other benefits as well.

Making short-run adjustments

Change doesn't always mean a major alteration or addition to a company's benefits program. But the constant flow of new government regulations, increases in insurance premiums, and so forth can require periodic minor changes in the details of a plan's provisions or in the costs that must be passed on to employees. Good benefits planning must include a reliable system for taking care of these small changes, along with those that will have a greater long-range impact.

Measuring progress

Nothing that a company does to keep its benefits program up to date will work very well if it occurs in a vacuum. Whenever there has been a benefits change, it's particularly important that its success—or failure—be monitored in some reliable manner. A company needs a continuous stream of information as to exactly how well the introduction of a new or changed benefit has worked out.

Some benefits changes can be measured quite accurately. The success of a cost-containment program for health insurance can be determined by comparing the total dollar amounts of claims before and after the program—with allowance for the influence of inflation.

Again, feedback from employees is important. If a formal survey of employee attitudes was used before the change was inaugurated, it may be a good idea to follow up with a similar survey mechanism—questionnaire, panel discussion, focus group, or whatever—to find out whether the benefits change has had the hoped-for effects. Whether or not a change was instituted after some formal employee-feedback process, it's most important to obtain some reaction from employees, even if it must be informal in nature.

Keeping things running

Successful management of an employee-benefit program, of course, involves much more than the high drama associated with planning, developing, and introducing major alterations. Each element of a company's benefit program must be administered: signing up new employees; designing and distributing forms; filing claims; answering questions; explaining why claims have been denied; signing off on employees who leave; handling accounting and actuarial problems; and all the other essential, day-to-day responsibilities of an employee benefits department.

To the average employee, it's how well these jobs are done—how quickly a reimbursement is made, how well a simple question is answered—that sets the standards by which a benefits program is judged. (At the same time, of course, there's always the danger of getting *too* involved in all the housekeeping and losing sight of long-term goal setting and planning.)

Finally, the importance of regular communication with employees can never be underestimated—especially when changes are made in their benefits. As we shall see in Chapter 6, the success or failure of many a company's entire benefits program can depend, to very large extent, on just how well that program is explained to the employees.

HANDLING SPECIAL PROBLEMS

For many companies, there are some important additional aspects of benefits administration, beyond what we have already discussed. Many of these special problems fall into these three general categories:

LABOR NEGOTIATIONS

As we pointed out in Chapter 2, labor unions have been responsible, in large part, for the rapid growth of some benefits. In particular, benefits that provide a large number of fairly small claims to a broad group of employees—such as dental and prescription-drug plans and supplemental unemployment insurance—have been particularly popular with the unions.

This impetus, of course, dates from the not-so-far-off days when the general feeling was that compensation of any kind, and especially benefits, would increase. That dream world has disappeared, and the emphasis is in the other direction. Organized labor is exerting less pressure to have business expand benefits into any more new (and expensive) areas. Instead, unions today are much more concerned with maintaining what they have already gained. Understandably enough, any "give-back" of benefit will be acceptable only after difficult negotiations.

A benefit plan, therefore, can end up as a pawn in a much bigger labor-versus-management game. The outcome can have serious effects on the company's entire benefits program for all its employees, union and nonunion. For a benefit plan that union members must surrender after a hard-fought battle is not likely to survive long for anyone else.

INTERNATIONAL BENEFITS

Administration of international benefits could be the subject of a complete book in itself. Obviously, it's a matter of extreme importance for corporations that have employees in a number of different countries.

There are a host of variables to be considered—in national differences, company size, type of industry, etc.—and therefore we shall not attempt to treat this highly specialized subject. However, here are a few important questions to ask about international benefits:

- Should American citizens working overseas receive the same benefits program as the company's domestic employees?

    A quick (and obvious) answer is, "Yes, of course." However, American benefits (for many reasons) are often radically different from those in other countries. Many Western democracies have become accustomed to extensive programs of social insurance, often involving government-sponsored health, retirement, child-care, and other benefits programs. In some of the developing countries, on the other hand, benefits are rudimentary or virtually nonexistent. When expatriate Americans must work alongside their foreign counterparts, these differences in benefits may present problems.
- So a related question could be: Should foreign nationals in overseas offices get the same benefits as American employees? And, continuing on: What do you do about third-world nationals?

Here the practice is relatively clear-cut. Most companies find it easiest to follow the benefits pattern of the local area, rather than getting involved in a complicated array of differing benefits.
- What happens when people move from one country to another?

Expatriate employees of an international company are often assigned to a series of different countries, and it can be awkward to keep changing their benefits program as they move from one country to the next. Sometimes there's nothing else to be done, since each nation may have its own pattern of legally required benefits that must be provided, whether a company wants to or not.
- And what about expatriates returning to the U. S.?

Sometimes this can be the rudest benefits shock of all. A middle manager returning home from a European office, where a free national health plan, long vacations, company-paid child-care leave, and a company car are customary, may find even the most generous American benefits program something of a disappointment.

Mergers and acquisitions

Another potentially traumatic situation, as far as employee benefits are concerned, will almost inevitably arise when two companies merge or when one acquires another. Almost certainly, there will be major differences between the two companies' benefits programs.

There's no easy way to resolve this question, but possible solutions might be:

- To retain the separate identity of each company's benefits program. This solution is most practical if the acquired company is to be operated as a virtually independent subsidiary under loose control, with little direct contact between employees of the two companies.

- To put all employees into the same benefits program immediately. A merger creates a host of potentially serious problems for almost every employee involved, with benefits being only one of them. So this solution, difficult as it may be at the time, may be the simplest in the long run.
- To let employees of the acquired company keep their old benefits for a limited period, but gradually absorb everyone into a single program. Merging two different benefits programs isn't always easy, and sometimes this is the best way to handle things. A number of sticky problems are created, of course, when two long-established defined-contribution pension plans must be melded into one; for example, how much credit, if any, do people get for their years of service under the old plan?

USING OUTSIDE HELP

When you're trying to do a good job of managing an employee-benefits program you may feel you can use all the help you can get. And help can come from many directions—although most of it, of course, carries a price tag. In Chapter 7 we list many of these benefits resources, including:

Benefits consultants. There are a host of them, ranging in size from individual practitioners to the consulting arms of the largest accounting, actuarial, and management-consulting firms.

Financial institutions. The larger banks, insurance carriers, investment firms, and other such companies very often have departments specializing in employee benefits.

Industry groups and associations. These range from lobbying organizations to nonprofit benefits research institutions.

Educational programs. Training courses in the fundamentals of benefits and topical seminars for professionals in the field are widely available.

Publications. A number of periodicals and full-length books are devoted exclusively to the field, and articles on benefits topics appear regularly in the business press and, increasingly, in general news publications.

Government bodies. The government isn't always the enemy of employee benefits—although sometimes it may seem that way. Many governmental agencies distribute useful publications and are good sources of up-to-date information about individual benefits programs.

6

COMMUNICATING EMPLOYEE BENEFITS

We've now come to the point where we must branch off and concern ourselves with something a little different from employee benefits themselves: how to discuss them with the employees for whom the benefits were designed.

This process of *benefits communication* has become, over the years, an industry unto itself. In this section we shall talk about the vital importance of benefits communications; the audiences at which it is aimed—who they are and when they should be talked to; the various legal requirements that affect what is communicated; and, finally, the various media that can be employed in doing this all-important job. Then, to sum up, we shall present a few basic principles that should be kept in mind by anyone communicating employee benefits information.

THE IMPORTANCE OF BENEFITS COMMUNICATION

To anyone who has followed our discussion of employee benefits this far, it might seem that the importance of communication is self-evident. Why go through all the trouble and expense of setting up the best possible program of benefits for a company's employees if these people never find out about it?

Amazingly enough, however, some companies persist in spending seemingly limitless dollars on benefits but only a few pinched pennies on communicating these same benefits. This just doesn't make sense, since the cost of even the most lavish communications program (and one need not go that far, of course) will be only a fraction of the cost of the benefits program itself.

The disparity between the cost of benefits and the cost of benefits communication becomes even greater as a company's size increases. Many of the basic expenses of a communications program (such as, for example, consultants' fees, photography, typography, and design) are fixed, regardless of the gross number of employees covered by the program. So, the more these fixed charges can be divided up, the lower will be the per-employee cost.

WHAT COMMUNICATION CAN DO

The general objectives of a company's benefits-communication program will, quite naturally, be very closely allied with the way that company looks at benefits themselves. As we discussed earlier, although every company's viewpoint will be unique, there are really two very broad approaches that can be taken toward employee benefits, and these will have a strong influence on how a company makes use of benefits communication.

If the benefits-as-need-fillers viewpoint predominates, communications will probably take a straightforward approach, clearly explaining what the various benefit plans are and how they can be used. If the benefits-as-added-compensation viewpoint is more important, communications will probably try to do more than simply present the facts, and will also try to sell the strengths and unique features of the company's program to employees.

When communication is most important

Whichever general communications attitude holds sway, it is especially important to let employees know about their benefit plans at certain specific times. These include:

When new employees join a company. This is the most vital time for effective benefits communication. It's one of the occasions when people are interested in hearing about their benefits. For once, they will sit still to hear everything they are told about the full range of their new company's benefits program. It may all come too fast for much detailed information to sink in, but at least there's the chance to create a positive feeling about the program in general.

Proper orientation of new employees is most important, but it's something that, all too often, companies do in a hasty and slapdash manner. But giving complete information about benefits is an essential portion of any well-thought-out orientation program. Above all else, it shouldn't be just handing new employees a set of benefits books and getting their hasty signatures on some forms they have barely had time to glance over.

Few people will decide to work for a particular company only because of its outstanding benefits reputation. But benefits can contribute to this decision—which means that newly hired employees will have a special interest in discovering whether all they have been hearing about their new company's benefits is true or not.

When new benefit plans are introduced. Sometimes, in the rush to design and perfect a new program, communication can be overlooked. This can be a disaster, since any new benefit must face a difficult audience—one that may not be so easily convinced of the new plan's virtues. Many employees are automatically skeptical of *anything* that's new in the benefits area; a company must accept this, and not expect employees to recognize instantly and accept without question all the wonders of a new benefit. If each detail is not carefully spelled out, this innate resistance to change may *never* be overcome.

When major changes are made. The announcement of important changes in established benefits will face the same skeptical audience. Many employees will view any alteration in long-familiar benefits unenthusiastically. Even when the change may seem (to management, at least) to be an unquestionable improvement, there will always be some employees who have their doubts. It's important to keep this danger in mind, and not to go overboard in selling the change to employees. They should be told why the change was made and exactly what it will mean to them.

When cutbacks must be announced. This is probably the hardest communications job of all. No one enjoys having to give bad news. And anything that appears to be a reduction in a company's benefit program will be greeted with instant resentment—even if it involves a benefit that was rarely used. Here it's best simply to bite the bullet and present the facts honestly.

When corporate developments affect benefits. A major change in a company's business activity sometimes can have important effects on employee benefits. This shouldn't be ignored in the rush to take care of everything else. A merger or acquisition may have serious consequences for a company's pension plan; a disastrous financial year certainly won't help the profit-sharing plan; even moving corporate headquarters from one state to another may necessitate a change in government-required benefits. Let the employee know what's happening.

A continuing job for communications

Don't assume that benefits communications is always part of a crash program of some sort; it shouldn't go into action only when major announcements must be made.

The best kind of benefits program is one that works well, day after day, without always calling attention to itself. But this routine competence can sometimes, ironically, be a disadvantage. If employees are to appreciate their benefits program, they should receive a steady flow of positive information. This might remind them, perhaps, of their less-publicized benefit plans; or call attention to especially large claims payments; or explain how to fill out forms; or point out the investment choices that can be made (and how they are doing currently). Benefits communication, in this way, can be most helpful to the employee—and good publicity for the benefits program in general.

However, there will be some times. . . . .

When communication is NOT all that important
Sometimes it's better to keep a low profile. If employees are subjected to a constant flood of news about minor changes in benefit plan provisions, minuscule rate increases, or routine reminders of deadlines, they'll begin to lose interest. And, with eyes glazed over from all this relatively unimportant detail, they won't recognize something really important when it does come along.

WHAT THE LAW REQUIRES

Whatever a company may *want* to do about benefits communications, it doesn't have a completely free hand. Some legal requirements govern communications, most of which date back to the Employee Retirement Income Security Act of 1974 (ERISA). When ERISA was originally passed there was a great hue and cry about the onerous requirements that the government was putting upon poor, helpless benefits managers throughout the country. (Plus, it must be said, gleeful anticipation by consulting firms of all the forthcoming communications business.)

Things haven't worked out quite as expected. Meeting the prescribed communications requirements hasn't been as difficult as many pessimists had feared. There are, of course, a good number of technical reports that must be filled out by benefit-plan sponsors and submitted to various governmental agencies. But, as far as employee communication is concerned, it boils down to three things that companies must distribute periodically to some or all of their employees: the summary plan description (SPD), statements of benefits, and the summary annual report (SAR).

The law says that a summary plan description of all "welfare plans" must be given to newly eligible employees and to all other plan beneficiaries. If any changes at all are made in a benefits program, a new edition of the SPD must be distributed every five years (or once every ten years even if there have been no changes). Certain employees are entitled to up-to-date statements of their status under some benefit plans. And summary annual reports of all a company's benefit plans must, as the name implies, be distributed once a year to employees covered by those plans.

SUMMARY PLAN DESCRIPTIONS

The authors of ERISA certainly had good intentions. They realized, as we have been pointing out here, that it's most important for employees to understand exactly what their benefits program covers—and doesn't cover. Although most of the act's provisions apply to pension plans, the communications requirement covers all "welfare" plans, which include most of the conventional employee benefits, such as health care, life insurance, and long-term disability plans. (To be on the safe side, most companies go ahead and include just about all benefits in their summary plan descriptions—the familiar "benefits booklets.")

The law provides considerable leeway as to exactly what must be said about each benefit-plan. Again, to be safe, it's a simple matter to mention somewhere in the booklet that readers must refer to a plan's legal documents for the final word on anything they don't understand.

One legal requirement, unfortunately, is violated with great regularity. It states that a benefit plan description should be "written in a manner calculated to be understood by the average plan participant." Of course, no one can be sure who an "average participant" is. And, by the time the copy in a typical benefits booklet has passed through the hands of the company's benefits consultants, its lawyers, and its personnel management, what remains, with great good luck, *may* be understandable to that average participant, whoever he or she is. But, more often than not, it won't be.

The usual summary plan description also must include some items that appear with great regularity: technical data about each plan, such as its official name and number, and some legalistic language telling employees what they can do if they think they have been ill-treated. (Almost always, this information appears in the boilerplate wording that has been helpfully supplied by the government.)

It must be noted that the Department of Labor has been less than stringent in overseeing the wording of summary plan descriptions. (One can imagine a giant warehouse crammed with all the unread booklets that have accumulated in Washington since ERISA's regulations went into effect.) However, the very existence of the regulation has exerted a certain amount of discipline on companies that, in pre-ERISA days, were doing a particularly poor job of benefits communication.

BENEFITS STATEMENTS

Each employee who is covered by a plan that changes in value has the right to know the status of his or her account as time goes by. Although most benefits statements are required only if employees ask for them, it's common practice to prepare and distribute them anyway—perhaps because much of the information they contain is of particular interest to a company's top executives.

Benefits statements are necessary for retirement plans, thrift and savings plans, and profit-sharing plans, where credits accumulate or the value of invested funds goes up or down. Employees also must be told when they will be vested under a retirement plan. And, if they leave a company with vested credits under such a plan, their employer must tell them exactly how much these total. Most employees, obviously, have a growing interest in how their stake in a plan is doing from year to year, and long-term employees can feel very comfortable if they know they have amassed a handsome amount of profit-sharing dollars or could now retire on a generous company pension.

However, these reports can be a two-edged sword. When times are difficult, it's never pleasant to tell employees that their carefully built-up investment in company stock is now worth significantly less than it was a year ago.

SUMMARY ANNUAL REPORTS

These are by far the least important or interesting of the required benefits communication documents. In theory, it's probably useful for employees to know the financial status of each of their benefit plans—if nothing else, to reassure them that these aren't about to go belly-up. Although there are exceptions, most companies seem to do only the legally required minimum. Each year, figures are plugged into standard "boilerplate" wording supplied by the government, copies are ground out for each employee, and most of the reports probably soon find their way to the nearest wastebasket.

HOW TO COMMUNICATE

Every sponsor of a benefits plan is required by law to prepare and distribute the documents we have just discussed. And it's very tempting, particularly for a smaller company, to do nothing more than the required minimum. That would be a mistake. Despite the reservations we have expressed, a summary plan description *can* be an informative, well-presented introduction to a company's benefits program. But a booklet, by its very nature, tends to be rather static. It can't keep employees current on recent changes. And it tends, once received, to be filed and forgotten—and referred to only when a question comes up about the specific details of one plan or another. To be effective, benefits communications must go beyond what is legally necessary.

Once this reasoning is accepted, the question is how to do the job. Almost any means of employee communication can be used for benefits communication, and the media that have been employed in this way, successfully and unsuccessfully, are numerous. For convenience, we shall divide them into three broad categories: printed publications, audiovisual presentations, and personal communications.

PRINTED PUBLICATIONS

Aside from the three legally required publications we have mentioned, there are many other possible ways of using the written word to communicate information about benefits. And, of course, today we are no longer confined to the conventional printing press; modern technology allows us also to use computer-printed publications of various kinds.

Here are some possibilities:

Typed memos or letters

A simple, very inexpensive way of distributing up-to-date information about changes in benefits, etc. When distributed desk-to-desk or sent through the company mail, these usually get most people's attention, at least for the moment. When sent to employees' homes, they'll probably be read by other family members—if that's the objective. And, with the help of word processing and lightning-fast laser printers, they can be individualized with ease.

Bulletin-board notices

Their use depends on the individual company. When employees are in the habit of getting important information from bulletin boards, they can be effective; elsewhere, bulletin-board notices may gather dust along with the obligatory minimum-wage postings and diagrams of fire exits.

Membership cards
Simple enough. But an official card with the title of a benefit plan and an employee's name on it is a communications medium nevertheless—perhaps the only one employees will actually keep in their possession all the time.

Pay envelope stuffers
Some companies are fond of these, but the number of people who actually read them is debatable. When did you last read the stuffers that came with your telephone bill?

Internal publications
Benefits information can be an effective regular feature of a company's internal newsletter, newspaper, magazine, or whatever else is published and distributed regularly to all employees. In addition to news of benefits changes and developments, these publications can include other kinds of benefits information, such as case histories of outstanding claims, question-and-answer columns on benefits, and the like.

Benefits summary folders
Much less elaborate than the periodically required summary plan descriptions, these can give a once-over-lightly glimpse of a company's benefits program. They can serve as satisfactory stopgaps between printings of the more complete booklets and can be passed out to prospective employees with recruiting brochures.

Specialized benefits publications
In theory, this sounds like a fine idea. Why not publish a regular newsletter entirely devoted to employee benefits? The big problem is that there usually isn't that much interesting news to persuade employees to read such a publication regularly. Only a large company with a very elaborate, dynamic benefits program might find enough to talk about.

Annual reports to employees

These have become popular with a growing number of companies—especially those that are extra sensitive to good internal communications. A summary of the year's progress in employee benefits should certainly take up a prominent part of any such annual report.

One-shot booklets

These make sense when an entirely new benefit plan is introduced—especially one that requires rather complete descriptive information, such as a 401[k] plan, new dental insurance, or, above all else, a flexible benefits program. But a booklet can't do the whole job of explaining a new benefit; its main purpose is to serve as a permanent compilation of information that employees may use for future reference.

Sliderules, wheels, and other gimmicks

A device that employees can slide or twist to see various numbers or words appear in window openings can pique their momentary curiosity. But it's doubtful whether these have enough permanent value to justify their fairly high production costs.

Inserts for looseleaf binders

Almost always, when a company is in the process of reprinting its benefits booklets—to meet summary plan description regulations or simply to bring them up to date—someone will suggest that a looseleaf binder be used. The usual argument for doing so is that future changes in benefits can be taken care of by reprinting and distributing selected pages for the binder. However, it's difficult to make sure that employees will take the time and trouble to insert new pages into their binders (assuming they still have them). In addition, printing individual pages is neither as easy nor as inexpensive as it might seem, and the binders themselves are never cheap. Sometimes it's simpler just to revise and reprint the whole booklet.

Individual benefits statements

These have grown in popularity over recent years, and a number of consulting firms now make a specialty of assisting companies in preparing them. The statements usually are computerized forms that are distributed each year to all employees, showing exactly how they stand in respect to a number of important benefits plans. Since the law requires that some of this information must be transmitted anyway, it makes a certain amount of sense to use this opportunity to remind employees of all the other benefits they have available to them. These statements often include some projections into the future, such as an estimate of an employee's pension at age 65, or a reminder of how much the company has invested in an employee's total benefits package during the past year.

Computerized statements have the special value of being one of the few kinds of benefits communication that can be completely individualized—that are aimed directly at the unique situation of each employee. And, especially the first time they are given out, they normally have a very favorable impact. Unfortunately, however, if they appear year after year in more or less the same format, they tend to be repetitive in what they say, and they seldom have the effect created the first time. So, considering the rather high cost—even if the job can be done in-house—a company might be well advised to reassess the value of this kind of communication on a permanent basis. Or, if nothing else, to take a fresh look at what it is doing, and not simply copy and update the old form, year after year. A benefits statement should give employees some interesting current information about their individual benefits—not just the same old facts and figures in the same old way.

AUDIOVISUAL PRESENTATIONS

These don't always have to be elaborate dog-and-pony shows. With the advent of computerized slide-making equipment and other new technology, a fairly impressive audiovisual production may not cost any more than a four-color printed booklet. But all such presentations share one advantage and one disadvantage when compared with the various printed media: They usually attract more attention and have greater *immediate* impact...but when they're over, they're over—nothing is left as a permanent reminder for the future.

Flip charts
Simplest, cheapest, and visually the least effective of all the possibilities. However, for a small audience they can be relatively useful. And they have one definitely positive feature: A live person must usually be there to flip the charts...and to elaborate on what they say.

Overhead projector slides
A variation on the above that is appropriate for larger audiences. They are less visually effective than conventional slides, but they have the advantage of not requiring a darkened room.

Slide shows
These can range all the way from a series of simple, homemade slides that clunk down as illustrations for a narrator's talk to multiprojector presentations with spectacular visual effects and stereophonic sound. Often, if they are carefully designed to fit a specific purpose, these can be very effective. But, sad to say, we live in a world of such sensational visual imagery today that many in a typical audience will not be overly impressed by even the most elaborate show. The costs, therefore, should be carefully weighed before plunging ahead with an expensive production of this kind.

Filmstrips
When equipment is available, these can sometimes be an effective part of an all-in-one audiovisual package for special purposes, such as a traveling presentation to introduce and explain a new benefit plan to employees in a number of small branch offices around the country.

Videotapes

With the proliferation of the video cassette recorder, these have become very popular for many internal communications purposes, and have also just about replaced the motion picture. Again, if the equipment is in place, videotapes can be effective for a number of special-purpose uses. Costs of production are still relatively high, however, even if a company has its own in-house facilities.

Television shows

Setting up television monitors in the employee lounge or cafeteria to present continuously running video shows to the passing crowd once seemed the wave of the future; now it's lost most of its novelty value. However, in a company where a significant number of employees are in the habit of watching these presentations, benefits communication can certainly be added to the menu.

Audiotapes

Not too long ago, in more innocent days, a recorded message from a top executive explaining a new benefit plan might have had some impact. Today, with almost every employee thoroughly used to visual stimulation, a disembodied voice alone probably has minimal value. A real, live person can be much more effective—even if it's only a lowly benefits analyst.

Recorded telephone messages

This is another scheme that often doesn't live up to its initial promise as an internal communication device. Setting up a special telephone number that employees can call to get the latest company information would appear to be relatively simple and inexpensive. The big problem, however, is finding enough interesting material to get people in the habit of calling this number regularly. However, if a company has succeeded in this difficult task, up-to-date benefits information can certainly be included among the recorded messages.

Computer-accessed information
This may *really* be the wave of the future: Employees gaining access to personalized benefits information via their own microcomputer terminals hooked into a central data bank, or individual diskettes prepared and distributed to employees. Only a few companies are utilizing such leading-edge communications right now, but who knows what the future will bring?

PERSONAL COMMUNICATIONS

Despite the many virtues of the various kinds of printed publications and audiovisual presentations, there really is no substitute for live, in-person communication. Employee benefits is a complicated subject that involves a lot of highly detailed information. Even the best publication or visual production must summarize, gloss over, and simplify to some extent. Yet benefits are very individual matters. Everyone is most concerned with how benefits work in his or her own situation—and, as we have pointed out more than once, almost everyone's situation today is likely to be unique.

Only when there is someone to answer individual questions can the benefits communication process really be complete; it can't be truly effective if it works in only one direction.

Formal presentations
To give the greatest impact to an important addition or change in a company's benefits program, there probably is nothing better than to hold a mass meeting of employees, with the news being announced by a top-level executive. The formal presentation will probably be backed up by an array of other communications—an audiovisual show, the distribution of new booklets, or anything else that seems appropriate. And a question-and-answer session could complete the package. These meetings have the greatest impact, of course, when the speaker appears in person before a live audience. However, when a company has widespread operations, such techniques

as *closed-circuit television* or *teleconferencing* may be substituted. It should go without saying that this kind of all-out effort must be reserved for the rare times when a benefits change is important enough to deserve this treatment.

Small group meetings

Of all the possible ways to communicate information about benefits, this is the one method that—if done right—is almost certain to be very effective. The groups of employees should be relatively homogeneous and small enough to allow informal, back-and-forth discussion of a new benefit, a change in a plan, or whatever. A series of group meetings, including all employees, often can carry almost the entire responsibility for benefits communication—or meetings can be used in combination with other printed or audiovisual efforts.

Most important to the success of these meetings, however, will be how well the people who run them are prepared. Meeting leaders must be thoroughly familiar with every aspect of the subject under discussion so that they can answer employees' questions accurately and with confidence. The only real problem with this kind of benefits communications, especially in a larger company, is one of logistics—training leaders, setting up meetings, seeing that all employees attend, and so forth. But the effort is almost always worth it.

Down-the-line communication

In some smaller companies, or those with strong hierarchical structures, the traditional form of communication may be down the line of command from manager to subordinate. If this is the way things work, benefits communication should follow the pattern—with the hope that messages don't become garbled along the way.

Personal counseling

All else being equal, individual, one-on-one discussion is unquestionably the most effective form of communication. However, except in the very smallest of companies, it's not a very practical way to transmit important benefits news. On the other hand, it's an excellent—perhaps even essential—way to make sure that employees understand, and use to their best advantage, a benefits program that is in regular operation. There will inevitably be individual problems that need special, personal attention. For these, the only real answer is to have at least one well-informed person (in a large company, it may even be an entire department) who always is readily available to answer questions, help employees fill out forms, track down missing checks, and so forth.

SOME BENEFITS COMMUNICATIONS PRINCIPLES

To sum up our discussion of benefits communications, the following are some important points to keep in mind, whatever the message may be and whichever media are chosen to get that message across to employees.

Assign permanent responsibility
Benefits communication is an important job. If done well, it can greatly enhance both the real and perceived value of a company's benefits program. But it's not something that should be done randomly. One person—or, in a large company, a department—must have the responsibility for communicating important benefits news when it occurs and, perhaps more importantly, reminding employees of their ongoing benefits on a day-to-day basis. Depending on a company's structure, benefits communications can be handled by any appropriate department: human resources, public relations, compensation and benefits, employee communications. The title doesn't really matter, but it should be *someone's* permanent responsibility.

Plan what you are going to say
Communication shouldn't take place in a shoot-from-the-hip manner. Before anything is said, the answers to some very

simple questions should be clear: What are we trying to say? To whom are we talking? What's the best way to get the message across? It's difficult to reach everyone with the identical communications media; you may decide to use different approaches with different employee groups or levels.

Explain everything very carefully

It's all too easy, especially for someone with long experience in the field, to underestimate how complicated benefits can be to an employee. Before any communication reaches the light of day, it should have a trial run with some typical employees, not just members of the benefits department. And remember, few employees are going to read a booklet straight through from beginning to end. Make it easy for them to find the specific information they are looking for.

Keep it simple

Very few employees have ever complained that the language in their benefits booklets was *too* simple. On the other hand, brevity is not always a virtue. It's better to explain everything in careful detail than to skip over something important just to save time and space.

Watch out for jargon

Like everything else, benefits has its own pitfalls to be avoided: buzzwords, acronyms, legalistic terms, and ordinary words that become jargon when they are used by the benefit community. A benefits manager may understand *exactly* what "continuous employment" or "credited service" means—but 99 out of 100 employees won't. Remember, you're not talking to the insurance company or the actuary or your lawyer—but to plain, ordinary people.

Reinforce the familiar

Employees shouldn't be expected to remember all the details of a benefit plan—even if it was carefully explained in that booklet they got in the mail last year. Benefits are not something the average employee spends much time thinking about—until the need arises. So a good communications program must not go into high gear only when big news is to be announced. It must also continuously reinforce employees' knowledge of what's already there.

Go beyond the printed word
We've already mentioned this more than once. Like it or not, many people today (especially those with limited education) are used to receiving most of their information from the visual media—not the printed page. Benefits communications must accept this fact of life and adapt to it. Simply passing out booklets at periodic intervals just won't do the job.

When you can, make it personal
Nothing hits home better than individualized facts and figures. Employees will understand and appreciate a benefit plan much more if they can see exactly what it means to them, rather than having to plow through a lot of general description or decipher the fine print of a chart. (This, of course, is one of the great virtues of the computer-printed individual benefits statement.) And don't expect employees to be greatly impressed when they're told how much money their company has spent on their benefits—especially when they haven't used them recently.

Anticipate resistance to change
Even if they don't know all the details of their benefits program, most people usually feel comfortable with what they have. Anything new will be greeted with a certain amount of skepticism, especially on the part of long-time company employees. And that holds true even if it's something that really is an obvious improvement.

Seek help when you need it
Benefits communication is not something for amateurs. Many companies *may* have all the talent they need on their own staff to do a perfectly satisfactory job. The only things you need, after all, are detailed knowledge of benefits, the ability to ex-

plain everything in understandable language, and thorough experience in every aspect of printed and audiovisual communications. On the other hand, it might be worth the extra cost to go outside for assistance. But remember that, in using an outside consultant, one trade-off must be made: broad knowledge and experience in the general area of benefits communications versus close familiarity with one company and its unique group of employees.

Respect employees' intelligence
If a benefit must be cut back for economic reasons, it's best to say so in plain English. Trying to pass off a much poorer plan as "just the same" as the one it replaces will fool no one. Benefits communication, like anything else, will lose most of its credibility if it isn't honest.

7
BENEFIT RESOURCES

Where do you go when you want help? To complete the full picture of employee benefits, these last pages list a number of sources of further information and assistance—plus a handy guide to deciphering some of the acronyms and abbreviations of which the benefits community seems to be so fond.

BOOKS

Many books on human resources administration, personnel management, compensation, and related subjects devote considerable attention to employee benefits. And a number of fairly technical volumes discuss such topics as pensions and Social Security. The following books cover the general field of employee benefits and are not intended primarily for specialists.

Beam, Burton T., Jr. and McFadden, John. *Employee Benefits*. Homewood, IL: Richard D. Irwin, Inc., 1985.

Foulkes, Fred F. *Employee Benefits Handbook*. Boston, MA: Gorham & Lamont, Inc., 1982.

Fundamentals of Employee Benefits Programs. 2nd ed. Washington, DC: Employee Benefit Research Institute, 1985.

Griffes, Ernest J. E. *Employee Benefits Programs.* Homewood, IL: Dow Jones-Irwin, 1984.

Mamorsky, Jeffrey, ed. *Employee Benefits Handbook, Annual Update.* Boston, MA: Warren, Gorham & Lamont, Inc.

McCaffrey, Robert M. *Managing the Employee Benefits Program.* Rev. ed. New York, NY: AMACOM, 1983.

Rosenbloom, Jerry S., ed. *The Handbook of Employee Benefits.* Homewood, IL: Dow Jones-Irwin, 1984.

―――. and Hallman, G. Victor. *Employee Benefit Planning.* Englewood Cliffs, NJ: Prentice-Hall, Inc., 1981.

PERIODICALS

The subject of employee benefits is one of ever-growing interest to business executives, and articles on the subject can be found regularly in the general business press, such as *Business Week, Dun's Business Month, Forbes, Fortune, Harvard Business Review, Nation's Business,* and *The Wall Street Journal.*

In addition, publications concerned with personnel management, such as *Personnel, Personnel Administrator,* and *Personnel Journal* have regular features and columns devoted to various aspects of benefits. And specialized publications now cover such subjects as health-care cost containment.

These publications, however, provide general coverage of the employee benefits field:

Benefits Quarterly
International Society of Certified Employee Benefit Specialists
P.O. Box 209, Brookfield, WI 53008

Benefits Today
The Bureau of National Affairs, Inc.
1231 25th Street N.W., Washington, DC 20037

Business Insurance
Crain Communications, Inc.
740 Rush Street, Chicago, IL 60611

Compensation & Benefits Management
Panel Publishers, Inc.
14 Plaza Road, Greenvale, NY 11548

Compensation & Benefits Review
American Management Association
135 West 50th Street, New York, NY 10020

EBRI Employee Benefit Notes and *Issue Briefs*
Employee Benefit Research Institute
2121 K Street N.W., Washington, DC 20037

Employee Benefit Plan Review
Charles D. Spencer & Associates, Inc.
222 West Adams Street, Chicago, IL 60606

Employee Benefits Journal
International Foundation of Employee Benefit Plans
P.O. Box 69, Brookfield, WI 53008

Nutshell
P.O. Box 5880, Snowmass Village, CO 81615

Pension World
Communication Channels, Inc.
6255 Barfield Road, Atlanta, GA 30328

Pensions and Investment Age
Crain Communications, Inc.
940 Rush Street, Chicago, IL 60611

ORGANIZATIONS

A variety of groups have been established for various special purposes, such as to represent the benefits community in Washington, to do research in the employee benefits field, to provide a regular flow of information to members and subscribers, and to sponsor educational and discussion programs. These are some of the leading organizations of these kinds:

American Association of PPOs
4301 Connecticut Avenue N.W., Washington, DC 20008

American Compensation Association (ACA)
6619 North Scottsdale Road, Scottsdale, AZ 85253

American Council on Life Insurance (ACLI)
1025 Connecticut Avenue N.W., Washington, DC 20036

American Management Association (AMA)
135 West 50th Street, New York, NY 10020

American Society of Pension Actuaries
1413 K Street N.W., Washington, DC 20006

American Society for Personnel Administration (ASPA)
606 North Washington Street, Alexandria, VA 22314

Association of Private Pension & Welfare Plans (APPWP)
1331 Pennsylvania Avenue N.W., Washington, DC 20004

The Bureau of National Affairs, Inc. (BNA)
1231 25th Street N.W., Washington, DC 20037

Chamber of Commerce of the United States (CCUS)
1615 H Street N.W., Washington, DC 20062

The Conference Board, Inc.
845 Third Avenue, New York, NY 10022

Council on Employee Benefits (CEB)
1144 East Market Street, Akron, OH 44316

Employee Benefit Research Institute (EBRI)
2121 K Street N.W., Washington, DC 20037

Employers Council on Flexible Compensation (ECFC)
1660 L Street N.W., Washington, DC 20036

ERISA Industry Committee (ERIC)
1919 Pennsylvania Avenue N.W., Washington, DC 20006

ESOP Association, Inc.
1725 DeSales Street N.W., Washington, DC 20036

Health Insurance Association of America (HIAA)
1025 Connecticut Avenue N.W., Washington, DC 20036

Institute for Management (IFM)
IFM Building, Old Saybrook, CT 06475

International Foundation of Employee Benefit Plans (IFEBP)
P.O. Box 69, Brookfield, WI 53008

International Society of Certified Employee Benefit Specialists
P.O. Box 209, Brookfield, WI 53008

Law & Business, Inc.
757 Third Avenue, New York, NY 10017

National Association of Suggestion Systems (NASS)
230 North Michigan Avenue, Chicago, IL 60601

National Center for Employee Ownership
927 South Walter Reed Drive, Arlington, VA 22204

National Employee Benefits Institute (NEBI)
2550 M Street N.W., Washington, DC 20037

National Institute of Pension Administrators
P.O. Box 15466, Santa Ana, CA 92705

National Small Business Association
1604 K Street N.W., Washington, DC 20006

Opinion Research Corporation (ORC)
P.O. Drawer F, Jamesburg, NJ 08831

Practising Law Institute (PLI)
810 Seventh Avenue, New York, NY 10019

Profit Sharing Council of America (PSCA)
20 North Wacker Drive, Chicago, IL 60606

The Research Institute of America, Inc. (RIA)
589 Fifth Avenue, New York, NY 10017

Risk and Insurance Management Society (RIMS)
205 East 42nd Street, New York, NY 10017

Self-Insurance Institute of America (SIIA)
P.O. Box 15466, Santa Ana, CA 92705

Society of Actuaries (SA)
500 Park Boulevard, Itasca, IL 60143

Society of Professional Benefit Administrators (SPBA)
2033 M Street N.W., Washington, DC 20033

Charles D. Spencer & Associates
   222 West Adams Street, Chicago, IL 60606

Washington Business Group on Health (WBGH)
   229-1/2 Pennsylvania Avenue S.E., Washington, DC 20003

EDUCATION

In addition to the many meetings, seminars, training courses, and conferences sponsored by the organizations listed in the previous section, special mention must be made of the *Certified Employee Benefit Specialist* program sponsored by the International Foundation of Employee Benefit Plans and the Wharton School of the University of Pennsylvania. Successful graduates of the program, after completing 10 college-level courses covering every aspect of employee benefits, receive the CEBS designation. The International Society of Certified Employee Benefit Specialists, open only to holders of the CEBS designation, sponsors a continuing education program, publishes a number of periodicals, and holds an annual employee benefits symposium.

GOVERNMENT AGENCIES

Sometimes the government itself can be the best source of information on many important aspects of employee benefits, and publications available through the Government Printing Office can often be most valuable. As it happens, benefits come under the jurisdiction of a number of branches of the federal government (in addition to all the state and local authorities), including:

Department of Health and Human Services
   200 Independence Avenue S.W., Washington, DC 20201

Social Security Administration
   6401 Security Boulevard, Baltimore, MD 21235

Department of Labor
   200 Constitution Avenue N.W., Washington, DC 20210

Bureau of Labor Statistics
   441 G Street N.W., Washington, DC 20212

Department of the Treasury
   1500 Pennsylvania Avenue N.W., Washington, DC 20220

Internal Revenue Service
   1111 Constitution Avenue N.W., Washington, DC 20224

National Credit Union Administration
   1776 G Street N.W., Washington, DC 20456

Pension Benefit Guaranty Corporation
   2020 K Street N.W., Washington, DC 20006

Small Business Administration
   1441 L Street N.W., Washington, DC 20416

United States House of Representatives
   —*Ways and Means Committee*
      —1102 Longworth Office Building, Washington, DC 20515

United States Senate
   —*Finance Committee*
      —19 Dirksen Office Building, Washington, DC 20510

BENEFITS CONSULTANTS

The ever-growing complexity of the employee benefits field means that it can be extremely difficult for any company to get along without help of some kind from outside. Assistance in setting up, improving, administering, and communicating about an employee benefits program is available from special departments of many of the leading insurance, accounting, and management-consulting firms.

In addition, a great many consultants today specialize in employee benefits. Smaller firms do business in most parts of the country, and following is an alphabetical list of the largest national benefits consultants with the addresses of their main offices; these firms also have branches in almost all of the larger American cities:

Buck Consultants, Inc.
   Two Pennsylvania Plaza, New York, NY 10121

Frank B. Hall Consulting Co.
   261 Madison Avenue, New York, NY 10016

A. S. Hansen Inc.
   1417 Lake Cook Road, Deerfield, IL 60015

Hay/Huggins Company, Inc.
   229 South 18th Street, Philadelphia, PA 10102

Hewitt Associates
   100 Half Day Road, Lincolnshire, IL 60015

Human Resource Management Group of
   Alexander & Alexander, Inc.
      1185 Avenue of the Americas, New York, NY 10036

Johnson & Higgins Human Resource Consulting
   95 Wall Street, New York, NY 10005

Kwasha-Lipton
   2100 North Central Road, Fort Lee, NJ 07024

William M. Mercer-Meidinger, Inc.
   1211 Avenue of the Americas, New York, NY 10036

Martin E. Segal Co.
730 Fifth Avenue, New York, NY 10019

Towers, Perrin, Forster & Crosby
245 Park Avenue, New York, NY 10167

The Wyatt Co.
1050 17th Street N.W., Washington, DC 20036

A SHORT GLOSSARY OF BENEFITS ACRONYMS AND ABBREVIATIONS

The benefits community has, over the years, been affected by a flood of laws, organizations, new benefit plans, and the like—many of which have come to be known almost exclusively by their initials. Some of these groups of letters conveniently, or by clever design, form pronounceable acronyms. In any case, following is a list of some of the more common ones. Most of them have been mentioned at one place or another in these pages, as the index will indicate.

(For a much more complete listing, see the annual publication *Employee Benefit Plans: A Glossary of Terms*, published by the International Foundation of Employee Benefit Plans.)

ACE	average current earnings (Social Security)
AD&D	accidental death and dismemberment
ADEA	Age Discrimination in Employment Act of 1967
AIME	average indexed monthly earnings (Social Security)
APB	Accounting Principles Board
ASO	administrative services only
BC/BS	Blue Cross/Blue Shield
BLS	Bureau of Labor Statistics
CAPP	cash account pension plan
CEBS	Certified Employee Benefit Specialist

CMP	competitive medical plan
COB	coordination of benefits
CODA	cash-or-deferred arrangement
COLA	cost-of-living allowance
COLI	corporate-owned life insurance
CPI	Consumer Price Index
CREF	College Retirement Equities Fund
DEFRA	Deficit Reduction Act of 1984
DI	Disability Insurance (part of Social Security)
DOL	Department of Labor
DRG	diagnosis-related group
EAP	employee assistance program
ERISA	Employee Retirement Income Security Act of 1974
ERTA	Economic Recovery Tax Act of 1981
ESOP	employee stock ownership plan
FASB	Financial Accounting Standards Board
FICA	Federal Insurance Contributions Act
FSA	Fellow, Society of Actuaries
FSA	flexible spending account
GAO	Government Accounting Office
GIC	guaranteed investment contract
HCFA	Health Care Financial Administration
HHS	Health and Human Service (U.S. Department of)
HI	Hospital Insurance (part of Social Security)
HMO	health maintenance organization
IPA	individual practice association
IRA	individual retirement account
IRC	Internal Revenue Code
IRS	Internal Revenue Service
ISO	incentive stock option
J&S	joint and survivorship
JCAH	Joint Commission on Accreditation of Hospitals
LOS	length of stay
LTD	long-term disability
MPPAA	Multiemployer Pension Plan Amendments Act of 1980
NRD	normal retirement date

OASDHI	Old Age, Survivors, Disability, and Health Insurance
OASDI	Old Age, Survivors, and Disability Insurance
OASI	Old Age and Survivors Insurance
PAT	pre-admission testing
PAYSOP	payroll stock ownership plan
PBGC	Pension Benefit Guaranty Corporation
PEPPRA	Public Employee Pension Plan Reporting and Accountability Act
PIA	primary insurance amount (Social Security)
PPO	preferred provider organization
PPS	prospective payment system
PRO	peer review organization
PSRO	professional services review organization
R&C	reasonable and customary
REA	Retirement Equity Act of 1984
RIPA	Retirement Income Policy Act of 1985
RFP	request for proposal
SAR	stock appreciation rights
SAR	summary annual report
SBLI	Savings Bank Life Insurance
SEP	simplified employee pension
SERP	supplemental executive retirement plan
SMI	Supplementary Medical Insurance
SNF	skilled nursing facility
SPD	summary plan description
SSA	Social Security Administration
STD	short-term disability
SUB	supplemental unemployment benefit
TCN	third-country national
TDB	temporary disability benefits
TDI	Temporary Disability Insurance
TEFRA	Tax Equity and Fiscal Responsibility Act of 1982
TIAA	Teachers Insurance Annuity Association
TPA	third party administrator
TRASOP	Tax Reduction Act Stock Ownership Plan
U&C	usual and customary
UCI	unemployment compensation insurance

UCR	usual, customary, and reasonable
VEBA	voluntary employees' beneficiary association
WC	workers' compensation
ZEBRA	zero-based reimbursement account

INDEX

accidental death and dismemberment (AD&D) insurance, 66-70
adverse selection, in flexible benefits, 166
adoption assistance, 127
air travel, special, 154
airplanes, company, 153
American Can Company, 158, 173-174
asset recovery, by terminating pension plans, 92-94
attitude surveys, employee, 202-204
automobile insurance, 130

benefits, employee
 administration, 2, 199, 212
 basic principles, 13-14
 cafeteria, see flexible benefits
 communication, see communication, employee
 and demographics, 11-12
 distinctions in, 186-190
 and the economy, 204
 educational programs in, 212, 239
 employees' sharing costs of, 183-186
 employment-related, 135-147
 entitlement to, 186-190
 feedback from employees on, 201
 for executives, 147-154
 flexible, 155-178
 funding of, 194-197
 goals, 3-8, 205-206
 and government, 201
 government-required, 135-137
 history of, 10-11
 international, 209-210
 and labor unions, 7, 10, 22, 47, 128, 137, 208-209
 management, 2, 199-212
 in mergers and acquisitions, 210-211
 objectives, 3-8, 205-206
 planning, 204-208
 and population changes, 11-12
 publications, 212, 233-236
 self-funding of, 195-197
 taxation of, 180-183
benefits consultants, 200, 211, 240-242
benefits statements, 219-220, 224

cafeteria plans, see flexible benefits
cafeterias, company, 145
car pooling, 142
cash-or-deferred arrangements (CODAs), 109-115
child care, 123-127
clubs
 employee, 146
 executive memberships, 153
coalitions, employer, 42
communication, employee
 audiovisual presentations, 224-227
 on health insurance cost containment, 42-44

individual benefits statements, 224
 informal channels of, 204
 legal requirements, 217-220
 methods of, 220-229
 personal, 227-229
 printed publications, 221-224
 upward, 204
commutation assistance, 141-142
company cars, 153
compassionate leave, 27
compensation
 deferred, 148
 executive, 148
consulting firms, 200, 211, 240-242
coordination of benefits (COB), 34
cost containment, health insurance, 38-44
 employee communication on, 42-44
cost-of-living increases, pensions, 90-91
costs
 employees' sharing of, 183-186
 health insurance, 33-34, 38-44, 47-48
 pension plans, 85-86
 Social Security, 117, 120
counseling
 financial, 152-153
 preretirement, 120-122
credit unions, 142-143

day-care centers, 126
de minimus fringe benefits, 135
death in family, time off for, 27
deductibles, health insurance, 34-35
defined-benefit pension plans, 80-91, 96-97
defined-contribution pension plans, 91-92, 98-112
dental insurance, 51-54
diagnosis-related groups (DRGs), 41
disability, definition of, 75
disability insurance, long-term, 72-77
discounts, merchandise, 143-144
dividend units, 150
drug plans, prescription, 55-56

educational assistance, 131-134
educational courses, in-house, 133-134
educational leave, 28
educational programs, benefits, 212
Educational Testing Service, 158, 172-173
employee-assistance programs (EAPs), 59-60
employee clubs and activities, 202-204
Employee Retirement Income Security Act of 1974 (ERISA), 79, 92, 98, 201, 217-220

INDEX 247

employee stock ownership
plans (ESOPs), 104-106
examinations, physical,
56-58, 153
executives, benefits for,
147-154
expatriates, benefits for,
209-210

financial counseling, 151-152
flexible benefits, 155-178
 alternative approaches to,
  167-170
 American Can Company plan,
  173-174
 arguments against, 164-167
 choices, 162-163, 166-167
 communication, 164
 Educational Testing
  Service plan, 172-173
 future of, 177-178
 limited-area choice plans,
  169-170
 modular programs, 169
 Thomas Jefferson
  University plan, 174-177
 TRW, Inc. plan, 171-172
flexible spending accounts
 (FSAs), 168-169
flexible working hours, 126
food service, subsidized, 145
401 [k] plans, see cash-or-
 deferred arrangements
free admissions, 135
frequent-flyer programs, 154
funding of benefits, 194-197
funeral expenses, 62, 67

gifts, matching, 134
gifts to employees, 144-145
"golden handcuffs," 149
government bodies, assistance
 from, 212, 239-240
government-required benefit
 programs, 135-137

handicapped children, aid
 for, 127
health, employee improvement
 of, 43, 58-59-146
health insurance, 29-50
 coordination of benefits,
  34
 cost containment, 38-44
 cost sharing, 33-34, 47-48
 coverage, 32, 37-38, 48
 deductibles, 34-35
 forms, 46-47
 self-funding of, 31-32
health programs, employee, 146
health maintenance
 organizations (HMOs), 32,
 44-46
holidays, 24-26
hospital insurance plans,
 37-38

illness, family, time off
 for, 27
incentive stock options
 (ISOs), 150
Individual Retirement
 Accounts (IRAs), 88, 107,
 111-112
information and referral
 services, child care, 124-125
insurance
 accidental death and
  dismemberment (AD&D),
  66-67, 69-70
 automobile, 130

dental, 51-54
hospital, 36-38
liability, 131
life, 61-72
long-term disability, 72-77
property, 131
short-term disability,
 19-20
travel accident, 67, 70
vision care, 54-55
integration, pension plans and
 Social Security, 83, 88-89
interest-free loans, 153
Internal Revenue Code, 109,
 155, 158
Internal Revenue Service, 105,
 135, 139, 142, 153, 180
international benefits, 209

job sharing, 125
joint-and-survivor option,
 pension plans, 89-90
jury duty, 27

labor unions and benefits, 7,
 10, 22, 47,128, 137, 208-209
leave
 compassionate, 27
 educational, 28
 maternity, 28, 125
 military, 28
 unpaid, 28
legal sevices benefit plans,
 128-129
liability insurance, 131
life insurance, 61-72
 after retirement, 70-71
 coverage, extent of, 63,
  68-69
 dependents, 67-68
 for funeral expenses, 62
 tax treatment of, 65-66
living quarters, executive,
 153
loans, interest-free, 153
long-term disability (LTD)
 insurance, 72-77
lump-sum payments, pension
 plans, 96

marriage, time off for, 28
matching gifts, 134
maternity leave, 28, 125
Medicare, 41, 191-192
merchandise discounts, 143-144
mergers and acquisitions,
 benefits problems of, 210-211
military leave, 27-28
multi-employer pension plans,
 90-91

nonqualified stock options,
 149

Old Age and Survivors
 Insurance, see Social Security
"open window," 149
opinion surveys, employee,
 202-203
options, stock, 149-150
out-of-pocket limits, health
 insurance, 36

payroll-based stock-ownership
 plans (PAYSOPs), 103-104
Pension Benefit Guaranty
 Corporation, 92, 114
pension plans, 77-98
 costs, 85-86
 coverage, extent of, 79,
  83-84

248 INDEX

death and disability
  benefits, 89-90
defined-benefit plans,
  80-91, 96-97
defined-contribution plans,
  91-92, 98-115
  formulas for, 81
  integration with Social
    Security, 83, 88-89
  investment size, 79
  multi-employer plans, 90-91
  payment methods, 87-88
  portability, 114
  taxes on, 115
  termination of, 92-94
  vesting, 79, 84-85
performance bonuses, 148
performance shares, 150
performance units, 150
periodicals, benefits, 234-236
perquisites, executives,
  152-154
personal days off, 26
phantom stock, 150
philanthropy, 134-135
physical examinations, 56-58,
  153
pooling, car and van, 142
portability, pension plans,
  114
post-retirement benefits,
  70-71, 190-194
preadmission testing, 40
precertification, surgical, 40
predetermination, dental care,
  53
preferred provider
  organizations (PPOs), 42
preretirement planning
  programs, 120-122
prescription-drug programs,
  55-56
profit-sharing plans, 98-103
property insurance, 131
publications, benefits, 212,
  233-236

recreation programs, employee,
  146
relocation assistance, 138-139
restricted stock, 150
retirement
  age of, 86-87, 120
  benefits after, 70-71,
    190-194
  early, 87
  planning for, 120-122
retirement benefits, 77-122
  cost-of-living increases
    in, 90
  supplemental plans, 148-149

sabbaticals, 22
salary continuation, 18-19
savings plans, 106-109
second opinions, surgery, 41

Section 401[k] plans, see cash-or-
  deferred arrangements
Section 501[k] (9) trusts, 195
self-funding
  benefits, 195-197
  health insurance, 31-32
service awards, 147
short-term disability, 17-21
sick pay, 17-21
Social Security, 115-120
  cost-of-living increases,
    192
  death benefits, 62
  disability insurance, 74-75
  early retirement, 87
  integration of pension
    plans with, 83, 88-89
  taxation of benefits, 181
stock appreciation rights
  (SARs), 150
stock options, 149-150
stock-ownership plans, 103-106
stock purchase plans, 143
subsidized food service, 145
suggestion plans, 139-141
summary annual reports (SARs),
  220
summary plan descriptions
  (SPDs), 218-219
supplemental executive
  retirement plans (SERPs),
  148-149
supplemental unemployment
  benefits (SUB), 137
surgery, second opinions, 41
surveys, employee opinion and
  attitude, 202-203

Tax Reduction Act stock-
  ownership plans (TRASOPs),
  103
taxation of benefits, 180-183
Thomas Jefferson University,
  174-177
thrift and savings plans,
  106-109
time off, 16-29
travel accident insurance, 67,
  70
TRW, Inc., 158, 171-172
tuition reimbursement plans,
  131-133

U.S. Savings Bonds, 107
unemployment compensation, 136

vacation, 21-24
van pooling, 142
vesting, pension plans, 79,
  84-85
voluntary employees'
  beneficiary associations
  (VEBAs), 195

wellness programs, 43, 58-59
workers' compensation, 136-137